VIRGINIA PATRIOTS

Their Lives, Contributions, and Burial Sites

JOE FARRELL • LAWRENCE KNORR • JOE FARLEY

SUNBURY
PRESS ®

Mechanicsburg, PA USA

Published by Sunbury Press, Inc.
Mechanicsburg, Pennsylvania

SUNBURY
P R E S S

www.sunburypress.com

For information about special discounts for bulk purchases, please contact Sunbury Press Orders Dept. at (855) 338-8359 or orders@sunburypress.com.

To request one of our authors for speaking engagements or book signings, please contact Sunbury Press Publicity Dept. at publicity@sunburypress.com.

FIRST SUNBURY PRESS EDITION: July 2025

Set in Adobe Garamond | Interior design by Crystal Devine | Cover by Lawrence Knorr | Edited by the authors.

Publisher's Cataloging-in-Publication Data
Names: Farrell, Joe, author | Farley, Joe, author | Knorr, Lawrence, author.
Title: Virginia patriots : their lives, contributions, and burial sites / Joe Farrell Lawrence Knorr Joe Farley.
Description: First trade paperback edition. | Mechanicsburg, PA : Sunbury Press, 2025.
Summary: The individuals from Virginia who played prominent roles in the founding of the USA are detailed.
Identifiers: ISBN 979-8-88819-321-1 (softcover).
Subjects: HISTORY / United States / Revolutionary Period (1775-1800) | BIOGRAPHY & AUTOBIOGRAPHY / Political.

Designed in the USA
0 1 1 2 3 5 8 13 21 34 55

For the Love of Books!

Contents

Introduction

Virginia has been the birthplace of great leaders. While other states claim the sites of great battles, the seats of government, or the places of protest, Virginia is known for its stately homes and storied leaders. Yes, the Revolutionary War ended at Yorktown with the brave charge of Redoubts 9 and 10, and Williamsburg was the site of many great debates and speeches, but the essence of Virginia today can be found at Mount Vernon, Monticello, Montpelier, and others.

We must start this book with George Washington, the Commander-in-Chief and first President of the United States. We were honored to be allowed into his tomb, which was opened for us by the National Park Service.

Thomas Jefferson follows, the great intellectual, thought leader, diplomat, and third President of the United States.

Then James and Dolley Madison, he contributing the U.S. Constitution, and she the bipartisan hospitality that helped keep the young republic together, especially when challenged by the War of 1812.

James Monroe, the fifth President of the United States, is the fourth chapter and the final member of what has been dubbed the Virginia Dynasty, which began with Jefferson.

The following chapters then progress alphabetically with no attempt at any further hierarchy. Great military leaders such as George Rogers Clark, Henry "Lighthorse Harry" Lee, and Daniel Morgan are in these pages. As are great politicians such as Patrick Henry, Richard Bland, Peyton Randolph, George Wythe, and George Mason.

Virginia is not without its great backwoodsmen such as the transplant Daniel Boone and Charles Scott, both of whom played large roles in the formation of neighboring Kentucky.

Other Lees and Randolphs appear here, including Richard Henry Lee, who made the motion for independence, Congressman Francis Lightfoot Lee, and Edmund Randolph.

The great Chief Justice John Marshall hailed from Virginia and laid the foundation of the Supreme Court in the early republic.

All told, thirty great Patriots from Virginia fill the pages of this book. While they are not close to the total of all persons who sacrificed or contributed in some way to the cause, they represent those most prominent or famous or who gave the most.

Please enjoy the retelling of our founding through the brief biographies of these citizens of Virginia. Always remember: "Poor is the nation that has no heroes, but poorer still is the nation that having heroes, fails to remember and honor them." (attributed to Marcus Tullius Cicero)

Lawrence Knorr, Ph.D.
June 2025

George Washington
(1732–1799)

Cincinnatus Americanus

Buried at Washington family crypt,
"Mount Vernon" plantation, Mount Vernon, Virginia.

———•—•———

Continental Association • Commander in Chief • Military
U.S. Constitution • First President of United States

George Washington was a surveyor and soldier from a privileged Virginia
family who rose to become the Commander in Chief of the Continental
Army during the American Revolution and the first President of the
United States. Dubbed "Father of Our Country," Washington was instrumental in leading the rebellious colonies to victory on the battlefield
despite long odds and few supplies. He then held the young republic together through his nonpartisan approach during the formation of the new
government following the adoption of the United States Constitution.
The nation's capital and hundreds of other places and streets are named
for him.

———≫•≪———

George Washington was born February 22, 1732 (new calendar), on
the family estate "Wakefield" near Popes Creek in Westmoreland County,
Virginia. He was the eldest of six children of Augustine Washington and
his second wife Mary (née Ball) Washington. George, Samuel, Elizabeth
(Betty), John Augustine, and Charles were siblings who survived to adulthood. Augustine was a wealthy planter, justice of the peace, and county

Portrait of George Washington by
Gilbert Stuart, circa 1797.

sheriff who also had four children by his first wife Jane Butler. Only two
of them survived to adulthood giving George two elder half-brothers:
Lawrence and Augustine.

When George was three, the family moved to "Epsewasson," a plantation on the bluffs of the Potomac River. Three years later, the family moved
to "Ferry Farm" near Fredericksburg where Washington spent most of his
boyhood. It is this farm that was the location of the Parson Weems cherry
tree legend. When George was 11, in 1743, his father passed away. He
became the owner of "Ferry Farm" but was raised by his elder half-brother
Lawrence at "Epsewasson" which was renamed to "Mount Vernon" in
honor of British Vice Admiral Edward Vernon under whom Lawrence
had served. Lawrence had married into the wealthy Fairfax family that
same year, taking fifteen-year-old Anne Fairfax as his bride.

As a youth, Washington had private tutors and learned the art of surveying. Due to his brother's connections with Lord Fairfax, young George had many opportunities to utilize his surveying skills and became a land investor as a teenager. Also, due to his brother's service in the Virginia militia, George became interested in the military. In 1751, Lawrence became ill with tuberculosis. The two made a trip to Barbados with the hope the warm air would cure him. While there, George contracted smallpox but survived. This immunized him but left him with scars on his face. Unfortunately, Lawrence was not cured and passed away after returning to "Mount Vernon" in July of 1752. Nine years later, when his sister-in-law passed, George inherited "Mount Vernon."

Soon after his brother's death, George took his place in the Virginia militia, being named adjutant for the southern district of Virginia by Governor Robert Dinwiddie. Through 1758, he fought in the French and Indian War, including rallying the retreat of the ill-fated Braddock Expedition. In time, Washington rose to the head of the Virginia militia but in December 1758, he resigned his commission and returned to "Mount Vernon." He then married Martha Dandridge Custis, on January 6, 1759, a wealthy widow with two children, John Parke Custis and Martha Parke Custis, whom he raised as his own. George and Martha had no children of their own. The marriage also greatly increased his wealth and social standing.

George shelved the military life for a while and began a political career. He was a member of the Virginia House of Burgesses from 1758 to 1774 and a justice of the peace from 1760 to 1774. As the Revolution neared, he was elected to the First Continental Congress and was reelected to the Second. During this time, he signed the Continental Association and on June 14, 1775, following Lexington and Concord, was asked to serve as the commander of all continental forces. Washington appeared humbled by this appointment, thanking Congress for the opportunity but cautioned he was not experienced enough or prepared for the task. He graciously accepted, eschewing a salary and asking only his expenses to be paid. The Continental Congress chose capable subordinate officers to assist, including Major General Artemas Ward, Adjutant General Horatio Gates, Major General Charles Lee, Major General Philip

Schuyler, Major General Nathanael Greene, Colonel Henry Knox, Colonel Alexander Hamilton, Colonel Benedict Arnold, and Brigadier General Daniel Morgan.

Washington took command of the army on July 2, 1775, at Cambridge, Massachusetts. He was astonished by how poorly prepared and undisciplined they were. He set about to correct these deficiencies. That September, he sent Arnold and 1000 troops to Canada to aid General Montgomery's siege of Quebec. The British reinforced the city, and the siege collapsed, forcing the Americans to retreat. Meanwhile, Washington proposed an attack on Boston, but his war council advised against it. He sent Henry Knox to retrieve cannons from the recently captured Fort Ticonderoga and had them placed on the Dorchester Heights in February 1776. General Howe then evacuated Boston.

Washington next moved his army to New York to fortify it, correctly predicting it would be the place of the next British attack. Howe resupplied in Nova Scotia and then headed to New York City. The two battled on Long Island in August, leading to another American retreat, this time under cover of darkness and fog to Manhattan. Washington considered abandoning Manhattan too, but generals Greene and Putnam urged him to defend it. Once again, Howe was victorious. Washington retreated to White Plains.

While Howe decided to stay in New York City for the winter, Washington crossed the Delaware into Pennsylvania as numerous enlistments were expiring and many were deserting. Howe split his army, placing a Hessian garrison in Trenton, New Jersey, to counter Washington's encampment. During Christmas of 1776, Washington launched a surprise attack on Trenton. He had boats gathered from up and down the river and then crossed the Delaware in heavy sleet and snow. At 8 AM on the 26th, the army attacked Trenton, surprising the Hessians there. Over 850 prisoners and supplies were taken and the Hessian colonel, Johann Rall, was killed. The Americans returned to Pennsylvania to consolidate their winnings and then headed back across the river on January 3rd, attacking British regulars at Princeton. Over 273 British were killed or captured to only 40 Americans killed or wounded. Washington himself led a counterattack coming within 30 yards of the British line. Howe's army retreated to New York City. Washington moved to Morristown, New Jersey, and camped for the winter.

Washington's home at Mount Vernon (photo by Lawrence Knorr).

The victories in New Jersey bolstered Washington's standing with Congress and led to many reenlistments. While in Morristown in early 1777, Washington had his army inoculated against smallpox. When British General Burgoyne moved south from Quebec to cut off New England, Howe decided to take Philadelphia instead of going up the Hudson to meet Burgoyne. At Brandywine, near Philadelphia, in September of 1777, the British outmaneuvered Washington and marched into Philadelphia. A subsequent attack on the British garrison at Germantown failed. Meanwhile, in upstate New York, General Gates defeated Burgoyne at Saratoga thanks to the aggressiveness of Generals Benedict Arnold and Benjamin Lincoln. This led to the resignation of General Howe in May 1778 and brought the French into the war on the side of the colonies.

Now Washington found himself in a precarious position referred to as the Conway Cabal. Some in Congress wanted to replace Washington with Gates and several generals were involved in the intrigue. He ultimately survived this challenge and wintered with his army at Valley Forge in December 1777. Washington petitioned for more supplies for his men while the cold winter weather raged and many died from illness and starvation. Five congressmen came to visit the situation and by February 1778, supplies were in hand and the situation was improving.

In May 1778, with the alliance with France in place, the British retreated from Philadelphia and headed back to New York. Washington decided to attack them as they retreated, resulting in the Battle of Monmouth. British General Clinton, now the leader of the force, rebuffed the attacks and garrisoned at New York City. This was Washington's last battle in the north. He put little value in conquering cities and saw his objective as preserving his army.

Late in 1778, Clinton sent troops to Georgia to launch a southern invasion. He seized Savannah and then Charleston in January 1780, defeating General Lincoln. Clinton returned to New York and put General Cornwallis in charge. The British then moved deeper into South Carolina and routed Lincoln's replacement, Horatio Gates. Washington had recommended Nathanael Greene for the role, but Congress had disagreed. Now, they sent Greene, who proceeded to drag the British out in a costly campaign.

In the north, in the summer of 1779, Washington sent General Sullivan after the Iroquois, who were British allies. Sullivan routed the natives, the survivors fleeing to Canada. At Morristown, the winter of 1779–80 was harsh. While dealing with the deprivation of the cold winter, Washington was not aware that Benedict Arnold was betraying him. British spymaster John André had turned him earlier in the year. By the summer of 1780, Arnold hatched his plot to allow the British to take West Point, an important fort on the Hudson. That September, André was captured and the plot discovered. Washington offered the British André in exchange for Arnold, but they refused. Arnold became an officer in the British Army and André was executed at Tappan, New York, in October 1780. André had asked to be executed by firing squad, but Washington changed his mind to make an example of him. He was hanged instead.

As Greene was turning the tide in the south, Washington urged the French to join him in an attack on Cornwallis in Virginia in 1781. Washington feigned an attack on New York and headed south to the coast of Virginia. After the French naval victory in the Battle of the Chesapeake, the patriot forces trapped Cornwallis's army at Yorktown on October 19, 1781. Cornwallis failed to appear at the surrender, sending General Charles O'Hara instead. In response, Washington sent Benjamin Lincoln in his place.

The British then began a withdrawal from the colonies and the two sides started negotiating a peace treaty. By the fall of 1783, all the foreign armies were gone. Meanwhile, Washington's army was again in bad shape with the American treasury empty. Many soldiers were not paid and some of the officers considered a military coup. Known as the Newburgh Conspiracy, this unrest was put down in March 1783 as Washington got concessions from Congress. Washington later submitted his expenses for the war, totaling $450,000.

The Treaty of Paris was signed on September 3, 1783, officially recognizing the independence of the United States from Great Britain. On November 2, Washington disbanded his army and gave a farewell address to the troops. The British finally evacuated New York City on November 25, 1783. A little more than a week later, Washington bade farewell to his officers at Fraunces Tavern in New York City on December 4. Nearly three weeks later, on December 23, Washington resigned his commission before the Continental Congress which was convened in the Senate Chamber of the Maryland State House. Said Washington,

> I consider it an indispensable duty to close this last solemn act of my official life, by commending the interests of our dearest country to the protection of Almighty God, and those who have the superintendence of them, to his holy keeping.

Washington emulated the Roman consul Lucius Quintus Cincinnatus in relinquishing his military power to the state after victory. Historian Gordon Wood concluded it was "the greatest act of his life, the one that gave him his greatest fame." The Society of the Cincinnati was subsequently formed by Henry Knox with Washington as its first president. Upon resigning, Henry Knox took over as the new commander of the Continental Army. Washington then returned to "Mount Vernon."

Washington had been a proponent for a strong central government and was critical of the Articles of Confederation. When the Constitutional Convention was called in Philadelphia in 1787 to replace the Articles with a new Constitution, James Madison encouraged Washington to attend as a delegate from Virginia. His presence added legitimacy to the proceedings and he was named the president of the convention. Washington stayed out of any disputes and was non-partisan while others argued back and forth. When it came time to approve the Constitution for Virginia, Washington recused himself feeling it was inappropriate for him to vote for it when he was likely to be the first president.

In early 1789, the various states began ratifying the Constitution, but the March 4 deadline passed without a Congressional quorum to declare who had become President of the United States. Finally, there was a quorum on April 5 and the votes were counted on the 6th. Washington had been selected president and John Adams, with the second-highest vote tally, was to be vice president. Congressional secretary Charles Thomson rode to "Mount Vernon" to inform Washington.

Washington took the oath of office on April 30, 1789, at Federal Hall in New York City. Over 10,000 people attended the first inaugural parade as Washington arrived via coach escorted by a marching band and the militia. The oath was administered by Chancellor Robert R. Livingston. Washington then went about forming a government and setting many precedents including the preference of being referred to as "Mr. President" as opposed to "His Excellency" or "His Highness" as was common in royal courts. He selected Thomas Jefferson as Secretary of State, Alexander Hamilton as Secretary of the Treasury, Edmund Randolph as Attorney General, Samuel Osgood as Postmaster General, and Henry Knox as Secretary of War. In 1790, he moved the seat of government from New York to Philadelphia.

During his first term, political parties began to form and most of the government found itself in two camps led by Hamilton and Jefferson. Washington, though clearly in the Federalist camp allied with Hamilton, tried to stay above things and remain as nonpartisan as possible. Washington backed the concept of a central bank which was the subject of debate between the sides and led to a compromise that included moving the nation's capital to the shore of the Potomac River. He was planning to retire after one term but was concerned about the in-fighting and lack of stability in the government. Thus, he put himself up for re-election in 1792 and was elected unanimously in the Electoral College. Adams was again vice president.

Washington assisted in the planning of the new capital and even helped lay the cornerstone in 1793 for the U.S. Capitol. In 1794, he rode at the head of an army as it crossed Pennsylvania for the Pittsburgh area in response to the Whiskey Rebellion. His personal commitment to put down the tax uprising further helped solidify the central government. After General St. Clair's failure three years prior, on August 24, 1794, General Anthony Wayne defeated the Northwest Indians at the Battle of Fallen Timbers, opening the Ohio country for settlement. On November 19, 1794, the Jay Treaty was signed with Great Britain, avoiding war and normalizing trade between the two countries. This greatly angered France and subjected Washington to more criticism than he had ever received from the Jeffersonians.

As Washington neared the end of his second term, he was relentlessly assailed by his political foes and a largely partisan press. He regarded the press as a disuniting force that spread falsehoods and even referred to them as "diabolical." Washington's term ended on March 3, 1797, when he was replaced by John Adams, who had narrowly defeated Thomas Jefferson. His farewell address to Congress reinforced the need for a strong central government and urged his successors to stay out of foreign entanglements. He returned to "Mount Vernon."

For more than a year, Washington enjoyed managing his plantation including a new distillery. However, he began to grow restless, especially when the French privateers began seizing American ships in 1798. He wrote to Secretary of War James McHenry offering his services to President John Adams. On July 4, 1798, Washington was offered the role of lieutenant general in charge of the armies. He accepted the position and held it until his death 17 months later. It was largely a ceremonial position as he delegated most responsibilities to Alexander Hamilton and did not assume field command. There was no invasion of the United States, as was feared.

On December 12, 1799, Washington rode out in the sleet and snow to inspect his plantation. He arrived late for dinner and did not change out of his wet clothes. By the next morning, he had developed a sore throat but still went out to mark some trees for cutting. That evening the sore throat had worsened, but he was still in good spirits. The following morning, his condition worsened and he had difficulty breathing. Doctors were summoned to treat him, drawing blood and foregoing a tracheotomy that might have saved him. He told his doctors as he sent them out of the room, "I die hard, but I am not afraid to go." His death came swiftly and unexpectedly at approximately 10 PM on December 14. Martha was at his side. He was 67 years old.

George Washington was laid to rest in the family vault at "Mount Vernon" on December 18, 1799. It was mostly a private affair of close friends and family. Washington's good friend Henry "Light Horse Harry"

The Washington tomb at Mount Vernon
(photo by Lawrence Knorr).

Lee offered a eulogy on behalf of Congress. Said Lee, Washington was "first in war, first in peace, and first in the hearts of his countrymen." In his will, Washington freed all his slaves and directed that a new family vault be built at "Mount Vernon." This was finally completed in 1831. The following year it was debated in Congress that Washington should be buried in the capitol. However, on October 7, 1837, Washington's remains were placed, still in the original lead coffin, within a marble sarcophagus designed by William Strickland and constructed by John Struthers earlier that year. To this day, the outer vault has the sarcophagi of

George Washington's sarcophagus
(photo by Lawrence Knorr).

George and Martha Washington while the inner vault has the remains of other Washington family members and relatives.

Washington remains the most important figure in American history. He is now carved into Mount Rushmore and his name has been used for a state, the nation's capital, numerous counties, cities, townships, boroughs, streets, and ships. The Washington Monument, on the mall in Washington, D.C., was finally completed in 1885 in his honor.

During the bicentennial, on July 4, 1976, Washington was posthumously appointed to the grade of General of the Armies of the United States by Congressional resolution, effectively a six-star general. This restored his place as the highest-ranking military officer in U.S. history along with General John Pershing.

Thomas Jefferson
(1743–1826)

The Founder of the Virginia Dynasty

Buried at Monticello Graveyard,
Albemarle County, Virginia.

This founder had many talents and interests. He was an inventor, an architect, a scientist and a gifted writer. He served the nation in multiple roles, first as a member of the Continental Congress, then as Governor of Virginia, as the United States minister to France, followed by a term as Vice-President and finally as the third President of the United States. He was also the first of three Virginians elected to the highest office in the land. All three served two terms in what is known as the Virginia Dynasty. He is best known as the principal author of the Declaration of Independence. It is ironic that the man who put pen to paper and wrote, "We hold these truths to be self-evident: that all men are created equal; that they are endowed by their Creator with certain inalienable rights, that among those are life, liberty and the pursuit of happiness" was a slave owner. This contradiction has made him one of the more controversial founders in recent times. His name was Thomas Jefferson.

Jefferson was born on April 13, 1743, in Shadwell, Albemarle County, Virginia. His father was Peter Jefferson, a successful tobacco planter and surveyor. Like the majority of Virginia planters, he owned slaves to work his fields and as his wealth increased, he purchased more land and more slaves. His mother was Jane Randolph Jefferson, who came from one of

Thomas Jefferson

Virginia's most distinguished families. When Jefferson was fourteen, his father died, and the young boy inherited an estate of about 5,000 acres.

As detailed by Winston Groom in his work *The Patriots: Alexander Hamilton, Thomas Jefferson, John Adams and the Making of America* Jefferson's education began when he was a young boy. At the age of five, he was enrolled in a local English school and by the time he was nine, he was studying French, Latin and Greek under the tutelage of a Scottish clergyman. After his father's death, he was instructed on the classics by Reverend Maury. At the age of 17 he enrolled in the College of William and Mary in Williamsburg. Here, he met the law professor George Wythe, a man who would remain an influence on Jefferson until the day he died. After two years in college, he studied law under Wythe, who sponsored his 24-year-old student to be a member of the Virginia Bar in 1767. He also regularly attended sessions of the House of Burgesses where he heard Patrick Henry forcibly denounce the Stamp Act.

After successfully passing the Virginia Bar examination, Jefferson began to practice law. He specialized in land cases or what is today known as real estate law. He also took on several cases on behalf of slaves who were seeking their freedom. In these cases, he found little, if any, sympathy for his arguments in Virginia. In one case, he argued that "Everyone comes into the world with a right to his own person. This is what is called personal liberty and is given him by the author of nature . . . Under that law, we are all born free." The judge was not convinced and ruled against him.

In 1768 Jefferson began work on the mountain home he would call Monticello. He designed the home itself and guided the builders, which included some of his slaves. During this time, he also spent a considerable amount of time reading from his book collection. He was especially attracted to the ideas of writers that, as a group, became known as the Enlightenment. These writers abandoned the idea of absolute faith in popes and kings. Instead, they saw a world ruled by logic and science. Jefferson would promote these ideas for the rest of his days.

In 1770, Jefferson met Martha Wayles Skelton. He fell in love, describing her as "distinguished for her beauty, her accomplishments and her solid merit. In 1772, the couple was wed. The years they were married were one of the happiest periods of Jefferson's life, according to his biographer Dumas Malone. The marriage would last ten years until Martha's death and produce six children, only two of which, Martha and Mary, survived to adulthood.

As told by Fawn M. Brodie in her work, *Thomas Jefferson: An Intimate History*, eighteen months after they were wed, Martha's father died and she inherited, among other things, 135 slaves. These included Betty Hemings and ten of her twelve children. The majority of them became favored house servants. Betty herself was given a cabin, and Jefferson noted in his account book payments to Betty for "pullets" and "fowls," which indicated special treatment. Later, Madison Hemings would write of his grandmother, "She had seven children by white men and seven by colored—fourteen in all." Brodie also adds that Martha's father had fathered three of what were her half-white sisters.

During this time, the work continued on Monticello and its gardens which was noted by Jefferson in the Garden Book he kept to record the status of his agriculture. Here, he detailed what had been planted, and it was a long list that included plum, peach, cherry and apple trees. There were also cabbages, radishes, carrots, peas, beans and potatoes. He also planted grape vineyards used to produce what his biographer described as a "respectable wine."

His first written political work to be widely praised was in 1774, titled *A Summary View of the Rights of British America*, which provided directions to Virginia's delegated serving in the First Continental Congress. In the document, he maintained that while Virginia did not want separation from the mother country, he wrote that King George III was "no more than the Chief officer of the people, appointed by the laws, and circumscribed with definite powers to assist in working the great machine of government." The work appeared in pamphlet and was purchased by both George Washington and John Adams. While he was not listed as the author, it became known that he had authored the work that was a repudiation of Parliament's authority over British Americans. Adams called it "a very handsome public paper." It brought Jefferson to the attention of people throughout the colonies.

In the spring of 1775, the battles at Lexington and Concord not only resulted in "the shot heard round the world" but brought a total war with England closer to reality. As a direct result a Second Continental Congress met in Philadelphia that May. Jefferson represented Vigilante as one of that colony's delegates. Initially, this meeting produced what was called the "olive branch," which was sent to King George in hopes of avoiding an all-out conflict. The king was unimpressed and simply ignored it.

In August, Jefferson returned to Monticello to spend time with Martha, who was suffering from health problems. He was also greeted with the news that British Governor Dunmore had announced that any slave who would join the British army in the fight against the colonies would earn his freedom. This edict brought with it the fear of a slave uprising.

In late March of 1776, Jefferson's mother passed away as a result of a stroke. For weeks after, he battled depression, which he ultimately overcame. That June, he was back in Congress in Philadelphia, where the delegates were debating whether to negotiate with England or declare independence. While the debate raged, Congress agreed that a declaration should be drafted in case the result was a vote for independence. Jefferson was assigned to a five-man committee, including Benjamin Franklin, John Adams, Roger Sherman, and Robert Livingston, which were assigned the task of producing a draft document.

The committee assigned Jefferson the task of writing what would be his most famous work, The Declaration of Independence, according to A. J. Langguth, in his book *Patriots,* Jefferson never intended the work to be original. His rivals would point to his debt to other writers like John Locke. He was also clearly influenced by the writings of his fellow Virginian, George Mason. In a recent work by David Fleming, *Who's Your Founding Father: One Man's Epic Quest to Uncover the First, True Declaration of Independence,* the author argues that the Mecklenburg Declaration signed on May 20, 1775, in North Carolina, was plagiarized by Jefferson when he composed his far more famous declaration. While Jefferson may have utilized many of these sources, it was he who put pen to paper and organized the arguments for independence that achieved the goal of expressing what thousands of Patriot essays written by the likes of Samuel Adams, John Adams, and Thomas Paine had been grouping for.

On July 1, 1776, the delegates, with Jefferson's declaration ready, took up Richard Henry Lee's resolution that the American states declare themselves independent. John Dickinson rose and argued that independence should be delayed until the states were confederated, the boundaries of the new nation fixed and a pact could be reached with France. John Adams hoped that some other delegate would rise to answer Dickinson, but none did, so Adams rose and repeated the arguments he had long made favoring independence. By this time, nine of the thirteen colonies publicly favored independence. During the debate, a dispatch arrived from General George Washington reporting that the British were poised to attack American positions in New York. That alarm may have swayed the delegates that Adams's arguments had failed to convince, and on July 2, 1776, with no dissenting votes, Congress declared that the colonies were free and independent states. Had the vote gone the other way, Jefferson's work would have been long forgotten.

After the Declaration was approved, Jefferson angered many of his colleagues. Congress requested he accompany Benjamin Franklin to France to seek aid for the Continental Army. Since Jefferson spoke French, he was a natural choice. He refused and resigned his seat in Congress. At the time, his wife was pregnant and in poor health. She had a history of problems when it came to childbearing, and this obviously influenced Jefferson's decision. Jefferson never informed those in Congress of her condition. His wife suffered a miscarriage.

As noted in *Patriots*, John Adams accepted another term in Congress. On returning to public service, he was leaving his wife, Abigail Adams, for the sixth time. Adams was upset with Jefferson's choice, writing that the country was not yet secure enough "to excuse your retreat in the delights of domestic life."

Jefferson returned to public service when he was elected Governor of Virginia in 1779. By this time, the British army had turned their attention to the American South. They had gained control over Georgia and South Carolina and were now fighting in North Carolina. There was little doubt that Virginia would be their next target. It was at this point in 1780 when Jefferson reluctantly began his second term as governor. By 1781 Jefferson's biographer Dumas Malone would record that his personal problems and the affairs of Virginia were so great that "reading about them" became painful. In April, his wife gave birth to a daughter who died at the age of five months. In May, a British force led by none other than Benedict Arnold captured the city of Richmond.

By this time, British General Cornwallis had also entered Virginia. He set up his headquarters at Elk Hill, located about 40 miles from Richmond. Jefferson had considerable holdings at Elk Hill, which Cornwallis destroyed. The English commander eliminated all the crops, burned the barns, and took the cattle and hogs as well as any horse that could be of service. Those not capable of service, including young colts, were killed.

June 2 was the last day of Jefferson's second term as governor. With the British soldiers on the march against the outnumbered Patriots, the state treasury virtually empty, and the political situation verging on collapse, Jefferson chose not to run for another term. Cornwallis sent his favored Calvary officer, Banastre Tarleton, to search for Jefferson and other Virginia lawmakers. Jack Jones, a captain in the Virginia militia, rode to Monticello to warn him of the approaching British calvary. Jefferson sent his wife and two daughters to a friend's plantation. He then mounted his favorite horse and rode to a vantage point with a good view of Charlottesville. Using a spyglass, he saw that the city was filled with British cavalry. Jefferson rode off to join his family. The British arrived at Monticello within minutes of Jefferson leaving. They questioned slaves regarding where Jefferson had gone. They searched the house to no avail. They waited for eighteen hours, thinking he might return.

Jefferson, meanwhile, moved his family to Poplar Forest, another plantation he owned located about 70 miles south of Monticello. Here he waited until the danger passed when Washington arrived and defeated Cornwallis at Yorktown. Jefferson's critics and his political enemies would point to his fleeing the British as evidence of cowardice. Actually, the future president had acted prudently. It is likely that if the author of the Declaration of Independence had been captured, he would have been treated unkindly. He could have been sent to London to languish in the Tower of London or hanged.

After the American victory in the Revolution, a state delegate called for an investigation of the final months of the Jefferson administration. Jefferson believed Patrick Henry, who was by now a political opponent, was behind the call for an inquiry. The complaint centered on the ease with which the British had invaded Virginia. Jefferson responded in writing to questions posed by the General Assembly. In the end, he was exonerated.

On May 8, 1782, Jefferson's sixth child was born, a daughter named Lucy Elizabeth. Martha Jefferson was ill after the birth and was confined to bed. She died on September 6, 1782, with Jefferson at her side. Others at the bedside included a number of the house slaves, among them the nine-year-old Sally Hemings and the forty-seven-year-old Betty Hemings both of which had been inherited from Martha's father. Jefferson took the death hard. He went to his room, where he stayed for weeks. He followed that with hours riding on horseback. He had lost the woman he adored, and there was nothing he could do to change it.

In the fall of 1782, the Continental Congress renewed their plea for Jefferson to go to France to represent the new country. With Martha gone, he no longer felt restrained, and he welcomed the opportunity. He accepted and would head to Europe for the first time in his life.

In 1784, Jefferson sailed to France as Minister Plenipotentiary to the Court of Versailles, joining Benjamin Franklin and John Adams. He felt prepared. He spoke French; he had studied the culture and the French philosophers. He viewed his goal to diplomatically achieve important, lasting treaties with France on both the commercial and military levels. His view was that a strong partnership with France would protect the new country of the United States from any aggressive British moves or policies.

In his five years of service in France, his diplomatic efforts produced only two treaties, one with Prussia and the other with Morocco. He was also responsible for a Consular Agreement with France in 1789. He also attempted to deal with the Barbary pirates of North Africa, who were seizing American ships and citizens and then demanding ransom for their return. His experience here convinced him that only a war could respond to these actions.

In 1787 Jefferson was still in France witnessing the beginnings of the French Revolution, much of which he agreed with, while the Constitutional Convention was meeting in Philadelphia. George Washington sent Jefferson a draft of the Constitution that the gathering Washington presided over had adopted. While he found some of the provisions to his liking, he was concerned about the power given to the executive branch and the lack of a Bill Of Rights. Despite his misgivings, Jefferson wrote to his friend Madison, saying that if the states "approve of the proposed Constitution in all its parts, I shall concur in it cheerfully, in hopes that they amend it whenever they find it work wrong."

As the French Revolution evolved, so did Jefferson's view. As detailed by H. W. Brands in this work *Founding Partisans* in May of 1789, Jefferson wrote to his friend Madison, "The revolution of this country has advanced thus far without encountering anything which deserves to be called a difficulty. There have been riots in a few instances in three or four different places, in which there may have been a dozen or twenty lives lost. But nothing inordinate or worrisome to lovers of liberty."

Just three months later, after the fall of the Bastille, Jefferson would write to Maria Cosway, a married woman he fell in love with during his days in France, "We have been in the midst of tumult and violence.

The cutting off of heads is become so much a' la mode, that one is apt to feel in the morning whether their own is on their shoulders." By this time, Jefferson had been granted his request to return to America. He left Paris on September 27, 1789, and headed to the United States, a country now governed by the First Congress and the first president, George Washington. Jefferson was accompanied on his trip home by his daughters Patsy and Polly and the slaves James Hemings and his sister Sally.

In 1787, when she was 14 years old, Sally Hemings traveled to Paris with one of Jefferson's daughters. Once in France, she was legally free because slavery was illegal in that country. She worked for Jefferson as a paid servant. At some point during her 26-month stay in Paris, Jefferson began having intimate relations with Hemings, who was the half-sister of Jefferson's departed wife, Martha. Jefferson was thirty years older than Hemings. According to one of Hemings' sons, at first his mother had refused to return to America with Jefferson. He claims that Jefferson offered her extraordinary privileges and promised that her children would be freed at the age of 21. It was on this basis that she agreed to return to America.

Evidence that includes modern DNA analyses shows that Jefferson impregnated Hemings multiple times during their time together at Monticello. Many historians agree that Jefferson fathered six of her children. Four of these children reached adulthood and were freed when they reached their 21st birthday. Confirmation of Jefferson's relationship with Hemings has affected his standing with a number of historians and Americans in general. In a 2001 Gallup poll on the Greatest Presidents in American History, Jefferson received one percent of the vote.

The historian Henry Wiencek, among others, noted that Jefferson was not the reluctant benevolent slave owner that many scholars had painted him to be. He writes that Jefferson's early efforts relative to emancipation ceased once he realized that the profits from slavery enabled him to live an extravagant lifestyle and maintain his beloved Monticello. In *Who's Your Founding Father*, David Fleming quotes the Virginia abolitionist, "Never did a man achieve more fame for what he did not do." In a review of Wiencek's book, *Master of the Mountain: Thomas Jefferson and His Slaves*, the *New York Times* referred to Jefferson as the "Monster of Monticello." New York's city hall removed a statue of Jefferson, whose stature has certainly suffered in many corners in recent times.

Upon his return to the United States, Jefferson learned that President Washington had nominated him to serve as the country's first Secretary of State. Jefferson was unsure that he wanted the position, and he wrote Washington that he was concerned about "criticisms and censures of a public . . . sometimes misinformed and misled." He added that his preference would be to remain as an ambassador. Washington responded that he "knew of no person" better suited for the office. Jefferson accepted Washington's judgment and became a member of the nation's first cabinet.

As Secretary of State, Jefferson defined the responsibilities of American diplomats living abroad. He also played a major part in negotiating the Compromise of 1790 from Philadelphia to what would become the District of Columbia in exchange for the acceptance of Secretary of the Treasury Alexander Hamilton's financial plan. Jefferson quickly grew to view Hamilton as a political rival who wanted to place too much power in the executive branch. Jefferson believed this threatened to destroy the liberty that had been one by the Revolution.

While all may have seemed well within the cabinet, that was hardly the case. Winston Groom, in his work *The Patriots,* describes an evening when Jefferson invited his fellow cabinet members to his home. The after-dinner conversation turned to politics and the British form of government. Vice President John Adams said, "If some of its defects and abuses (of the British system) were corrected, it would be the most perfect Constitution of government ever devised by man." That comment appalled Jefferson, who wasn't made any happier when Hamilton said, " It was the most perfect model of government that could be found and that the correction of its vices would render it an impracticable government." That evening, Hamilton also noticed portraits hanging in Jefferson's dining room, and he asked his host who the men were. Jefferson identified Sir Francis Bacon, Isaac Newton, and John Locke, describing them as the three greatest men the world had ever produced. Hamilton replied, " The Greatest man . . . that ever lived was Julius Caesar." The evening convinced Jefferson that Hamilton and Adams intended to install a British style of government in America.

As time went on Jefferson grew not only to dislike his job but also living in Philadelphia. He also disagreed with President Washington's position that America should remain neutral relative to world affairs. Jefferson wanted to ally with France. Washington wanted Jefferson to stay on the job, but despite the president's wishes, Jefferson submitted his resignation on January 31, 1793. With reluctance, Washington accepted it on New Year's Day and offered "my most earnest prayers for your happiness accompany you in your retirement." John Adams didn't exactly share Washington's view, writing to his wife Abigail, "Jefferson went off yesterday and good riddance to bad ware." He added that he knew Jefferson had talents but that he believed "his mind is now poisoned with passion, prejudice and faction." Little did Adams know at the time that Jefferson would be his main rival in the next two presidential elections.

Jefferson returned to Monticello as the de facto head of the opposition party. He kept himself busy building his estate, tending his gardens and horseback riding. He also remained very interested in current affairs. His two protégés and future presidents, James Madison and James Monroe, carried on a steady correspondence with him dealing with the news of the day.

When President Washington announced that he would not seek a third term, Jefferson became the leading candidate of the Democratic-Republican Party for the highest office in the land. In August of 1796, he received a letter from Tennessee Senator William Cocke telling him that the people of his state wished him to be the next President, with New York's Aaron Burr serving as his Vice President. At the time, potential presidents did not campaign for the office only acknowledging their willingness to serve after others put their names forward. Jefferson's name was indeed put forward, and he found himself facing the Federalist candidate, John Adams.

In his farewell speech Washington warned against the factions forming in the country. His wish was not granted. The election of 1796 would be the first to pit two political parties against each other, and it would turn into a bitter fight. The Federalists painted Jefferson as a coward who had abandoned his post as Governor of Virginia during the Revolution and with the violence surrounding the French Revolution. This was false.

Meanwhile Jefferson's party was accusing Adams of favoring a monarchy. Federalists also accused Jefferson of being an atheist and being too pro-French. Jefferson's effort may have been hurt when the French ambassador publicly backed him shortly before the election. In a close election, Adams received 71 electoral votes, which was one more than he needed. Jefferson won 68 electoral votes and became the Vice President. Thus, we had two rivals elected to the highest offices in the land. It was clear that the founders had made an error in setting the election system, a fact that would become even clearer in the turbulent election of 1800.

Prior to the vote by the Electoral College, Madison had told Jefferson that the possibility existed that he would finish second and that he needed to be prepared to accept the Vice Presidency. That was fine with Jefferson, who said, "It is not the less true, however, that I do sincerely wish to be second on that vote rather than the first." On March 4, 1797, both Jefferson and Adams were inaugurated. On that day, Jefferson told Madison, relative to Washington, "The President is fortunate to get out just as the bubble is bursting, leaving others to hold the bag." Later at the White House, Adams told Jefferson that he wanted his participation in decision making. Remembering this conversation, Jefferson would later write, "He never after that said one word to me on the subject, or even consulted me on any measures of the government."

One of the reasons Adams may have decided to marginalize Jefferson was the Vice President's attitude toward the French nation, which remained favorable. That nation was a major problem, perhaps the only one Adams inherited from Washington. The French were preying on American merchant ships. In addition, France was at war with Great Britain and was upset that the Americans had signed the Jay Treaty with the former mother country. In addition, in a move Jefferson objected to, after the execution of Louis XVI, America decided to cease the repayment of Revolutionary War debts to France, saying the debt was owed to a different regime.

The tensions between the former allies became known in history as America's Quasi-War with France. At the time many were convinced it would turn into a real war. By July of 1798, Adams declared that the country needed to prepare to defend itself. Congress agreed and passed bills creating a standing army, which Jefferson opposed. In addition, the Marine Corps and the Department Of Navy were established. Funds were directed to build three twenty-two gun frigates with plans to build an additional eighteen warships. Jefferson favored these moves but not to fight France. He was convinced that he could win the presidency in 1800 and saw the warships as being necessary to defeat the Barbary pirates.

Pulitzer Prize author Edward J. Larson, in his work *A Magnificent Catastrophe*, described the election of 1800 as tumultuous and as America's first presidential campaign. It certainly was unlike any other, as we had a sitting President and Vice President in two different parties fighting to win the highest office in the land. The Federalist Party candidates were President John Adams and Charles C. Pinckney of South Carolina. The Democratic-Republicans nominated Jefferson and Aaron Burr from New York. While these were the candidates, another prominent American, Federalist Alexander Hamilton, would play a significant role in determining the election results.

The main issues included the effects of the French Revolution and the Quasi-War. The Federalists wanted to maintain close ties with England and were in favor of a strong federal government. The Democratic-Republicans wanted more power placed in the hands of the states and criticized the taxes the Federalists had levied. They also made the Alien and Sedition Acts that had been passed by the Federalists an issue. These acts made it more difficult for immigrants to become citizens and made it easier to prosecute those who were critical of the federal government.

On December 14, 1799, George Washington passed away. Both Washington and Hamilton had considerable influence on the Adams cabinet members. With Washington's death, Adams became more independent and, in Hamilton's view, too independent. As a result, Hamilton schemed, behind the scenes, to have Pinckney elected to the highest office in the land. Hamilton believed that Pinckney would be more open to his influence.

While Hamilton hoped his activities on Pinckney's behalf would only be known to fellow Federalists who shared his views, he made the mistake of writing a 54-page letter in which he made the case that Adams was unfit to hold the highest office in the land. The Democratic-Republicans obtained a copy of the letter and immediately began reprinting it in their newspapers. The letter, which showed that there were major divisions in the Federalist Party, became a major factor in the election. When the electoral votes were cast, Jefferson and Burr each received 73 votes compared to 65 for Adams and 64 for Pinckney. The tie resulted in the election being decided by the House of Representatives.

The Constitution required the House to wait until February 11 to begin casting ballots. In the weeks that led up to that date, there were rumors and intrigue. Jefferson's party feared that the Federalists would pass legislation that would place the Federalists in charge of the executive branch. According to Jefferson, he verbally informed Adams that a move to install a temporary executive would result in "resistance by force and incalculable consequences." In addition, some feared that the Federalists would make a deal with Burr to preserve some of their power and influence in return for making him president. Burr distanced himself from the fray, allowing things to take their course. The fact that he did not publicly endorse Jefferson may have contributed to Jefferson's distrust of his running mate.

The voting began with each state casting one vote, with the winner being the candidate securing a majority of the state delegations. Neither Jefferson nor Burr were able to gain a majority on the initial 35 ballots. Jefferson was winning the backing of the state delegations controlled by his party, but the Federalists were backing Burr. Once again, Alexander Hamilton played a large role in the outcome. He had a strong dislike of both men but preferred Jefferson. He believed that under either man, the country was heading towards disaster, and he believed his party would share in the blame if Burr were elected. Hamilton convinced several Federalists to change their votes, and Jefferson was elected on the 36th ballot.

On March 4, 1808, Jefferson's second cousin, Chief Justice John Marshall, swore him in as the third President of the United States. Taking office, Jefferson faced the challenge of dealing with the 83-million-dollar national debt. His Secretary of the Treasury, Albert Gallatin, developed a plan to eliminate the debt in sixteen years. Among the moves Jefferson made was a reduction in both the nation's army and navy. By the end of his two terms in office, the debt was reduced to $57 million.

Jefferson's crowning achievement during his first term was the Louisiana Purchase. He instructed James Monroe and Robert R. Livingston to negotiate with France to purchase New Orleans and surrounding areas. At the time, Napoleon needed funds to continue his wars. In April of 1803, he surprised the American negotiators by offering to sell 827,987 square miles of territory for 15 million dollars. The United States accepted the offer doubling the size of the United States. The purchase gave the country access to some of the most fertile land of its size on the planet. It also opened the door to westward expansion.

As detailed in Brian Kilmeade and Don Yeager's work, *Thomas Jefferson and the Tripoli Pirates,* Jefferson was the first President to go to war with a foreign country. From his days as Secretary of State, Jefferson had firsthand experience dealing with the North African Ottoman provinces of Algiers, Tunis, Tripoli, and the Sultanate of Morocco. Barbary corsairs and crews from these countries preyed on merchant ships in the Mediterranean, capturing their crews and either enslaving them or holding them for ransom. Jefferson had long opposed paying ransom or tribute, and when he became President, he was determined to address the problem.

After Jefferson was inaugurated, Yusuf Karamanli, the Pasha Of Tripoli, demanded payment of $225,000 from the United States. Jefferson refused to comply. The Pasha responded by cutting down the flagstaff in front of the American Consulate, which was the Barbary way of declaring war. The war would last until 1805. The decisive Battle of Derna resulted in the American flag being raised for the first time in victory on foreign shores. On June 10, 1805, Karamanli signed a treaty ending the hostilities.

In 1804 Jefferson ran for re-election, replacing Aaron Burr with George Clinton as his running mate. The Federalists nominated Charles Cotesworth Pinckney. Jefferson's party pointed to a very strong economy, the Louisiana Purchase, and lower taxes as the administration's achievements. Jefferson won in a landslide the vote in the Electoral College was 162–14.

Jefferson's second term was marked by difficulties due to the wars in Europe. The country's relations with England suffered, and the relationship between Jefferson and the British diplomat Anthony Merry contributed to the deterioration. In 1805 Napoleon became less cooperative relative to trading rights. Jefferson's response was the Embargo Act of 1807, which targeted both England and France. This act was largely both unpopular and ineffective and led to a drastic decline in exports. Jefferson abandoned the policy after a year.

Although Jefferson had replaced Burr in his second term, his dealings with his former Vice President were not over. Seeing he had no future with Jefferson, Burr ran for Governor of New York in 1804. He was

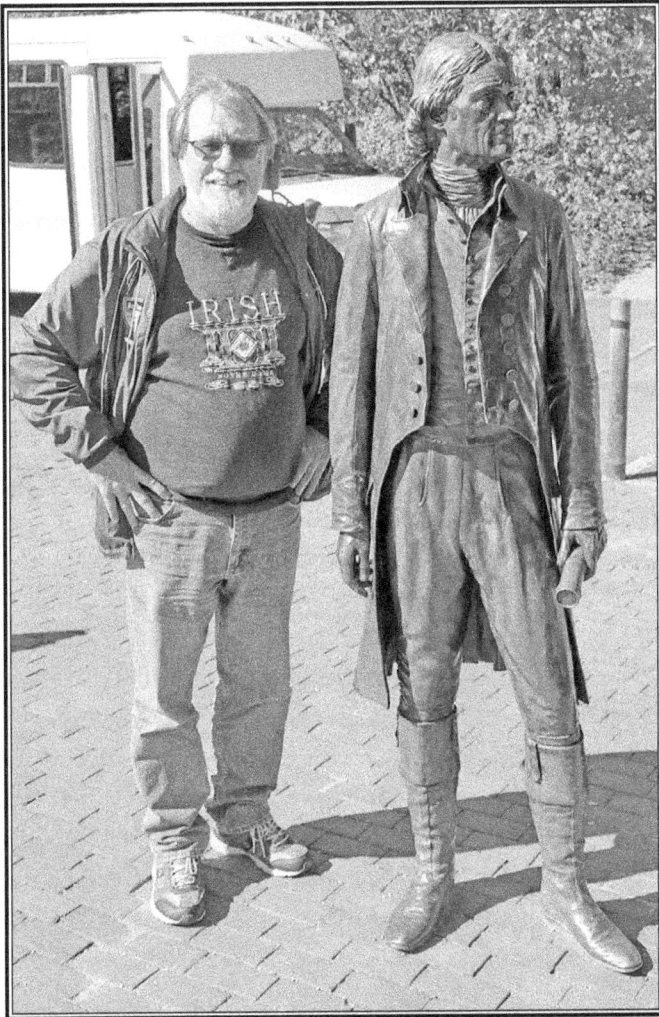

Joe Farley and Thomas Jefferson

soundly defeated. During the campaign, Alexander Hamilton made some disparaging remarks relative to Burr's character, and Burr challenged the former Secretary of the Treasury to a duel and mortally wounded him. Killing Hamilton effectively ended Burr's political career.

As detailed in the work of James E. Lewis Jr. titled *The Burr Conspiracy,* Burr set his sights on the western part of the country. In the fall of 1806, he and sixty men headed down the Ohio River. Historians differ on his intentions. Some say he had enticed supporters with a plan to liberate Spanish Mexico. Others with promises of land in the Orleans territory. There were rumors that his real intention was to establish his own empire in the western part of the country. Burr had consulted with the Louisiana Territory Governor James Wilkinson, who reported the plot to Jefferson. Jefferson ordered that Burr be arrested for treason. Burr was captured and sent to Virginia to be tried by a court presided over by John Marshall.

Reactions to the arrest and trial captivated many. John Adams, in a letter, remarked that he had never believed Burr to be a fool, but if he really was guilty of the accusation, he must be an "Idiot or a Lunatic." Senator William Plumer remarked that "Burr is capable of much wickedness, but not of so much folly." Some, including Adams, felt that if Burr were acquitted, he could still become president. He was indeed found not guilty, but his political career was over.

Jefferson was succeeded in office by two fellow Virginians, James Madison and James Monroe. He was said to be the founder of what is called the Virginia Dynasty. After he left office, he continued to correspond with both men. As a matter of fact, the Monroe Doctrine was influenced by the advice Monroe sought from Jefferson.

Jefferson spent his final days at his beloved Monticello. In July of 1825, his health began to deteriorate. By June of the next year, he was confined to his bed. On July 3, he was overcome by a fever, and he had already declined an invitation to attend an anniversary celebration of his Declaration. The next day, on the 50th anniversary, he passed away, with his last words being, "Is it the fourth?" or "This is the fourth." John Adams died later that same day. After Jefferson passed, a gold locket was found around his neck. It contained a lock of his wife Martha's hair. He was laid to rest at Monticello.

Grave of Thomas Jefferson

Since his death, Jefferson's reputation among historians has risen and fallen in cycles. Currently, it would be at low tide. Historians and many Americans have serious questions about how, as a slaveholder, he failed to live up to the words he had written in 1776. Not to mention that one current author in his book, *Who's Your Founding Father*, questions whether

Jefferson should be credited with writing the Declaration. As noted earlier, New York City removed a statute that had been erected to honor Jefferson. Things were far different in the 20th Century when Jefferson was selected to be one of the four presidents on Mount Rushmore. During those years, it was not unusual for the Democratic Party conventions to be decorated with gigantic posters depicting the man who founded their party. On April 29, 1962, President John F. Kennedy hosted a dinner at the White House honoring the Nobel Prize winners from the Western Hemisphere. Shortly into his welcome, Kennedy said, "I think this is the most extraordinary collection of talent, of human knowledge, that has ever gathered together at the White House, with the possible exception of when Thomas Jefferson dined alone."

James Madison
(1751 – 1836)

The Father of the Constitution

Buried at Madison Family Cemetery at Montpelier,
Montpelier Station, Orange County, Virginia.

———•◦•———

U.S. Constitution • Congress • 4th United States President

This founder played a pivotal role in both the passage and ratification of the United States Constitution. He was a co-author of *The Federalist Papers*. He also played a pivotal role in the drafting of the first amendments to the Constitution, known as the Bill of Rights. With Thomas Jefferson, he organized the Democratic-Republican Party to oppose the Federalist Party. When Jefferson was elected president, he served as his Secretary of State. During his tenure, he convinced Jefferson to submit the Louisiana Purchase Treaty to the Senate for approval. In 1808, he was elected to succeed Jefferson as president. He led the country through the War of 1812 and was reelected that same year. Historians rank him as one of the most significant founding fathers. His name was James Madison.

———▶◦◀———

Madison was born on March 16, 1751, at the Belle Grove Plantation in Virginia. His father was James Madison Sr., one of the largest landowners in the colony. The younger Madison was tutored by Donald Robertson, who was known for working with prominent families. In 1769, he enrolled at the College of New Jersey, now known as Princeton University.

James Madison

One of the main reasons Madison decided to study in New Jersey rather than at the College of William and Mary, like most college-bound Virginians, was due to his health. The Williamsburg climate was considered to harbor more infectious diseases. As detailed by Lynne Cheney in her work *James Madison: A Life Reconsidered,* Madison had suffered seizures during his childhood that are common in temporal lobe epilepsy. Cheney writes that based on the available evidence, this was the pattern "of Madison's ailment: fever-related episodes when he was a toddler, then sudden attacks later in life."

As related by Cheney, Madison did well enough on his Latin and Greek entrance exams to be able to skip his freshman year. During his sophomore year, he decided to complete his junior and senior studies concurrently. After he received permission to do so, he began what he described as "an indiscreet experiment of the minimum of sleep and the maximum of application which the constitution could bear." He earned his degree, but at a price. Dr. Witherspoon carried a letter to Madison's father, explaining that his son's efforts had led to a health crisis. Cheney maintains that it is reasonable to suppose that the crisis was described as "sudden attacks, somewhat resembling epilepsy." Madison returned to Virginia in a state of depression. Writing to a friend, he said, "… I think my sensations for many months past have intimated to me not to expect a long or healthy life." As it turns out, in this instance, Madison was mistaken, as he lived a long and fruitful life.

In 1773, 130 men disguised as Indians dumped thousands of pounds of tea into the Boston Harbor in what became known as the Boston Tea Party. While Madison agreed that Boston had been singled out for assaults by the British, he preferred what he called Philadelphia's more temperate approach. He wrote, "I wish Boston may conduct matters with as much discretion as they seem to do with boldness." He admired the conduct of those in Philadelphia and hoped to visit the city. He got his wish when his father decided to send his brother to a northern boarding school. Madison was probably in Philadelphia when the news arrived that the British had closed the Boston harbor. This action resulted in many Americans, including Madison, to harden their opinions due to these harsh tactics. He would make many more visits to Philadelphia in the years to come.

Madison's career in politics and government began in 1774 when he took a seat on the local Committee of Safety, a group that favored revolution. A year later, he became a colonel in the Orange County militia. Where he served under his father until he was elected as a delegate to the Fifth Virginia Convention, which led to the creation of Virginia's first Constitution. At the Virginia Constitutional Convention, he was instrumental in gaining the alteration of the Declaration of Rights, changing the word "tolerance" to "equal entitlement" in the practice of religion. He then became a member of the Virginia House of Delegates, where he formed a close friendship and strong alliance with Thomas Jefferson.

In 1779, Madison was elected to the Second Continental Congress. The historian J. C. A. Stagg described Madison as a legislative workhorse as he studied financial issues and coalition building. He was also a strong supporter of the American alliance with France and the country's westward expansion. After his term in Congress ended, he was elected to the Virginia House of Delegates in 1784. In this position, he, along with Jefferson, continued to support religious freedom. The two future presidents drafted the Virginia Statute for Religious Freedom. It passed in 1786 and resulted in the guarantee of freedom of religion, as well as the disestablishment of the Church of England.

During this period, Madison grew concerned about the weakness of the federal government established by the Articles of Confederation. He wrote, "A crisis had arrived which was to decide whether the American experiment was to be a blessing to the world, or to blast forever the hopes which the republican cause had inspired." In 1787, Madison was among the Virginians chosen to represent the state at the Constitutional Convention in Philadelphia.

Madison arrived in the City of Brotherly Love over a week before his fellow Virginia delegate, George Washington, made his much-anticipated entry. Washington's carriage was escorted by Philadelphia's City Troop and cheered by crowds as he made his way to the home of Robert Morris. Madison was more than pleased to see the hero of the Revolution because he knew that Washington's presence at the convention would be beneficial in securing the support of the people.

It took over a week for enough state delegations to arrive, allowing the convention to begin. The initial order of business was to elect a presiding officer, and Washington was the unanimous choice. In Madison's view, the gathering would "decide forever the fate of republican government." He was also determined to preserve a record of the proceedings for historical purposes. Therefore, he kept detailed notes on the remarks made by the delegates. In the evening, he would work long hours transcribing his notes, an arduous process that he would recall "almost killed him."

Clearly, Madison was very serious about the convention's success. Historian Clinton Rossiter, in his book *1787: The Grand Convention*, notes that Madison was one of the delegates who never missed a single session. Rossiter calls him the leading spirit and quotes Major Jackson, who called Madison the "most efficient member" in the conclave. The historian points to Madison's foresight in drafting the Virginia Plan and making it the agenda of the convention, his willingness to debate great issues and small with courteous and learned intensity, his dozens of suggestions of ways for his colleagues to extricate themselves from thickets, his membership on three of the four essential committees, even perhaps his doggedness in the major struggle for power—these are the solid credentials of the one Framer who stands, modestly and eternally, first among his splendid peers. Madison's performance at the convention has led many to call him the "Father of the Constitution."

On September 17, 1787, the delegates gathered to sign the finished product. Three delegates, George Mason, Edmund Randolph, and Elbridge Gerry, refused to sign the document. The Constitution was then sent to the states for ratification. Madison knew his work had only begun. Mason and Randolph were also from Virginia and were sure to oppose ratification at the state's ratifying convention. Their primary concern was that the Constitution did not include a Bill of Rights. Those who supported ratification were known as Federalists, and Madison was a member of this faction. Those opposed were known as Anti-Federalists.

The Anti-Federalists began a public campaign opposing ratification. In response, beginning in October 1787, two New York Federalists, Alexander Hamilton and John Jay, wrote a series of letters in support of ratification that appeared in New York newspapers. The letters or essays were published under the name Publius. When illness forced Jay to drop out of the effort, Hamilton approached Madison, who was in New York serving in Congress, to take his place. Madison agreed, and the trio produced 85 essays that became known as *The Federalist Papers*. The articles were published in book form and used by the Federalists in the state ratifying conventions. The work became highly regarded for its advocacy of representative democracy. The historian Clinton Rossiter wrote, "*The Federalist* is the most important work in political science that has ever been written, or is likely ever to be written, in the United States."

The Virginia Ratifying Convention convened on June 2, 1788, and Edmund Pendleton was elected to preside over it. By this time, Madison had convinced Edmund Randolph to support ratification, and the duo became the leaders of the Federalists. The Anti-Federalists, who would make most of the speeches during the convention, were led by Patrick

Henry and George Mason. When the convention began, both sides acknowledged that the outcome was highly uncertain.

Henry, who was widely known for his speaking ability, argued that the delegates in Philadelphia should only have suggested amendments to the Articles of Confederation. He said that the proposed Constitution would put an end to Virginia's liberty and the state government. Randolph, who had altered his position since refusing to sign the Constitution, argued that the confederation of states had proven to be totally inadequate and that if the Constitution was not ratified, the Union could well be lost.

Mason took the position that a national government would burden Virginia with direct taxes and that a government that rules such a vast territory would destroy liberty. He said he wanted a clear distinction between the powers of the federal and state governments, including the judiciary because shared authority would result in "the destruction of one or the other." Madison took the position that the history of Confederations was proved inadequate in the long run. He said the proposed Constitution would provide the country with a Republic, with each branch of the government grounded in the people.

On June 27, George Wythe put forward a motion to ratify. The motion passed 89 to 79, although Virginians reserved the right to withdraw from the new government. The gathering also recommended amendments, including the addition of a Bill of Rights. Patrick Henry's opposition never wavered. He refused to serve in the new government, turning down offers to serve as Secretary of State and as a justice on the Supreme Court. Using his influence over the Virginia legislature, he successfully made Virginia the only state to send two Anti-Federalist senators to the First Congress.

After serving in the Congress of the Confederation, Madison returned to Virginia and made an unsuccessful attempt to run for the U.S. Senate in 1788. At this point, he feared that Patrick Henry and the Anti-Federalists would arrange for a second constitutional convention. Against this background, he ran for a seat in the House of Representatives. Again, he was opposed by Henry, who recruited James Monroe to run against him. In the midst of this challenging race, Madison pledged to support constitutional amendments that protect individual rights. This promise was pivotal in his victory as he was elected to the First Congress, receiving 57 percent of the vote.

While there was no doubt that Washington would be the first president, who would fill the second spot was a question. Prior to the electors being chosen, Madison sent a ciphered letter to Thomas Jefferson. He expressed his dissatisfaction with the two most prominent names being put forward. He described John Hancock as "weak, ambitious, a courtier of popularity given to low intrigue." When it came to John Adams, Madison was convinced that his feelings of self-importance would doom him. In the same missive, he claimed he had always been in favor of a Bill of Rights. He took this position despite the fact that at the Virginia Ratifying Convention, he declared that supporting such a position was "dangerous because an enumeration which is not complete is not safe" and "unnecessary because it was evident that the general government had no power but what was given it." He now favored a Bill of Rights because he had made a promise to deliver it to get elected and because he would be the one framing it.

Madison studied more than two hundred amendments that had been proposed at the state's ratifying conventions. He then introduced a Bill of Rights on June 8, 1789. His proposal faced virtually no opposition. He had successfully quashed the Anti-Federalist goal of a second convention and, at the same time, avoided including anything that would alienate supporters of the Constitution. The ten amendments were ratified on December 15, 1791.

The country wasn't long into the Washington administration before political factions began to emerge. Alexander Hamilton led one faction that championed northern financial concerns and strong ties with Great Britain. This group became the Federalist Party. Thomas Jefferson and Madison led the other faction, which supported Southern interests and close ties with France, forming the Democratic-Republican Party. The two groups battled over Secretary of the Treasury Hamilton's financial plan. Among other things in the plan was the establishment of a national bank. Madison argued that the Constitution did not give Congress the authority to create such an institution. His argument failed; Congress voted to create the First Bank of the United States, and Washington signed the law in February 1791.

James Madison's house

Jefferson and Madison continued to oppose Hamilton by taking their positions to the people. They aided Philip Freneau in the founding of a Philadelphia newspaper, the *National Gazette*. In the fall of 1792, prior to the second presidential election, Madison wrote that the country had been divided into two distinct camps. On one side, some believed "that mankind are capable of governing themselves." He contended that the Federalists supported the creation of a class of aristocrats who would favor the wealthy. In the election that followed, both parties supported Washington, but the Democratic-Republicans made an unsuccessful effort to remove Adams as Vice President.

Jefferson and Hamilton had often clashed during Washington's first term. As told by Fawn Brodie in *Thomas Jefferson: An Intimate History*, Jefferson had concluded that his rival was impregnable. He decided to resign and return to Virginia. He submitted his resignation effective December 31, 1793. When Jefferson left office, Madison became the leader of the Democratic-Republican Party in Washington. When England and France went to war in 1793, the question was, who would the United States support? Madison favored France, while Hamilton favored England. When England began seizing American ships trading with French colonies, war with the mother country seemed imminent. Washington, looking to avoid a war he felt the young country was ill-prepared to fight, secured friendly relations with England through the

Jay Treaty of 1794. Madison's strong opposition to the treaty led to a break with Washington, ending their friendship.

On September 15, 1794, Madison married. The bride was Dolley Payne Todd, a 26-year-old widow. The couple had been introduced by one of New York's senators Aaron Burr. The couple never had children, though Madison adopted Dolley's son from her previous marriage.

After serving two terms, Washington decided to retire. In the 1796 election, Madison convinced Jefferson to run for the highest office in the land. The Federalists were supporting Vice President John Adams. This became the first presidential election in which competing parties vied for the presidency. The campaign was bitter as the Federalists identified the Democratic-Republicans with the violence of the French Revolution.

Meanwhile Jefferson's party accused the Federalists of favoring a monarchy. The Jay Treaty was also attacked as being too favorable to England. The Federalists countered by calling Jefferson an atheist who was a coward during the American Revolution. Adams won a close election, garnering 71 electoral votes to Jefferson's 68. Based on the Electoral College rules in place at the time, Jefferson became the Vice President because he had received the second-highest total of votes. Madison had declined to run for reelection and returned to Virginia.

Madison may have been out of office, but he was still a prominent leader of the opposition party. Both Jefferson and Madison held the view that the Federalists had violated constitutional rights by passing the Alien and Sedition Acts. Madison firmly believed that the acts set a dangerous precedent by giving the government the authority to disregard the rights of people in the name of national security.

With his election to the Virginia legislature in 1799, Madison made his return to office. At this point, he was also planning Jefferson's 1800 run for president. In that controversial election, the Federalists were divided between those who supported Adams and those who supported Hamilton. When Jefferson and his running mate, Aaron Burr, received an equal number of electoral votes, the election was decided by the House of Representatives. Jefferson was elected president, and Burr was elected vice president.

Despite his lack of foreign policy experience, Madison was appointed Secretary of State, where he wielded considerable influence in Jefferson's cabinet. It was in this position that he began to rely on Dolley Madison to manage the social demands of being a high-ranking public figure in Washington. She would fulfill that role throughout his life.

With the rise of Napoleon, Democratic-Republican support for France cooled. Madison pursued a position of neutrality relative to the conflict between the French and the British. In 1802, Jefferson and Madison sent James Monroe to France to negotiate the purchase of New Orleans, primarily due to the control of access to the Mississippi River. Napoleon countered with an offer to sell the entire Louisiana territory. Monroe, along with American Minister to France Robert Livingston, negotiated the Louisiana Purchase despite the fact that such authorization from Jefferson was lacking. Jefferson was concerned about the constitutionality of the purchase. He favored a constitutional amendment authorizing Congress to obtain territories. Madison convinced him that such an amendment was not required. The administration then submitted the Louisiana Purchase Treaty to Congress for approval without an accompanying amendment. In Madison's view, treaties between the United States and other countries were already authorized by the Constitution. Both houses of Congress quickly accepted the treaty.

During the Napoleonic Wars, Madison played a pivotal role in managing trade relations with both France and Great Britain. He viewed England as a significant problem due to their use of impressment, where they forcibly conscripted American sailors into the British navy. He attempted to negotiate a treaty with England that would protect American trade rights and prohibit the practice of impressment. Failing in this endeavor, he supported the implementation of economic sanctions against the British, including the Embargo Act of 1807. This act prohibited all exports to foreign nations. It was unpopular and very difficult to enforce, particularly in New England. Early in 1809, Congress replaced the Embargo Act with the Non-Intercourse Act, which permitted trade with nations other than England and France. The impressment issue was one he would inherit when he succeeded Jefferson as president.

By 1808, when the presidential election to select Jefferson's successor took place, the Federalist Party had collapsed. As a result, Madison's main opposition came from within his party, particularly from Congressman

John Randolph, who attacked Madison due to his association with the ongoing embargo. James Monroe and Vice President George Clinton challenged Madison for the Democratic-Republican nomination. Madison, with the strong backing of Jefferson, prevailed. He then easily defeated the Federalist candidate, Charles Cotesworth Pinckney, receiving 122 electoral votes to his opponent's 47.

As told by the historian Kevin R. C. Gutzman in *The Jeffersonians: The Visionary Presidencies of Jefferson, Madison and Monroe* Jefferson declined Madison's invitation to ride with him in his carriage to the inauguration. Jefferson explained the decision, saying, "I wished not to divide with him the honors of the day." Instead, Jefferson followed the carriage as a member of the crowd unattended on horseback. When he was directed to a seat near Madison, he also declined, saying, "This day I return to the people, and my proper seat is among them."

When Madison began his inaugural address, he appeared nervous, but he soon found his footing. He laid out a set of principles that would guide him. These included peace with nations that wanted it, neutrality toward belligerents, and diplomacy instead of war when practicable. Commitment to the Union and the Constitution, supporting the freedom of conscience and respect for individual rights, particularly the freedom of the press. He favored limitations on military spending during times of peace and a reliance on the militia. He wished to support agriculture, manufacturing, commerce, science and education. He said he would continue to convert the Indians from "savage" to "a civilized state." Gutzman concluded that Madison "would indeed hew to these principles as president, for good and for ill."

Jefferson, during his time as president, generally enjoyed unified support. Such was not the case with Madison. He would encounter political opposition from former allies, including Monroe. He had hoped to make Albert Gallatin his Secretary of State, but due to opposition, he kept him as Secretary of the Treasury. According to historians Ketcham and Rutland, his cabinet was chosen to promote political harmony but was unremarkable and incompetent. For example, he appointed Robert Smith as his Secretary of State, but due to Smith's incompetence, Madison found that he had to perform most of the duties of that office. Madison would replace Smith with Monroe in 1811.

In the early months of his presidency, Madison continued Jefferson's policies of low taxes and debt reduction. In 1811, he allowed the charter of the First Bank of the United States to lapse. Throughout his first term, he continued to struggle with both French and English attacks on American shipping. Hoping to pit those two countries against each other, he offered to trade with whichever country would cease their attacks. In 1810, Napoleon dictated a letter addressed to the American minister in Paris, offering to lift the Berlin and Milan decrees, which were the French justification for seizing American ships. This offer was conditioned on the British renouncing their blockades or on the United States, causing "their rights to be respected by the English." Madison accepted the offer, and as Cheney points out in her biography, critics at the time and since have noted this as a sign of Madison's gullibility. They questioned how Napoleon could be trusted. Madison wrote to Jefferson, saying, "We hope from the step the advantage of having but one contest on our hands at a time," adding, "The original sin against neutrals lies with Great Britain."

As told by Gutzman in his work on the period, a significant change occurred when Congress convened on November 4, 1811. It marked a generational shift in the American republic's leadership. Additions to the House of Representatives included Henry Clay of Kentucky and South Carolina's John C. Calhoun. These men were determined to confront England. In their time, Clay, Calhoun, and Daniel Webster were regarded by historians as more significant figures than all but a couple of presidents between James Monroe and Abraham Lincoln.

Madison delivered his State of the Union Address on November 5, 1811. He made it clear that, after years of patience with the two belligerents, he was at a breaking point. Madison's private secretary, Edward Coles, looking back on those days, told William Cabell Rives, a former U. S. senator and Madison biographer, "It was congenial alike to the life and character of Mr. Madison that he should be reluctant to go to war." However, Britain's decision demanding substantial concessions from the United States had "closed the door to peace in Madison's opinion."

With Britain embroiled in the Napoleonic Wars, many Americans, including Madison, believed the United States could easily capture

Canada and use it as a bargaining chip. On June 12, 1812, Madison asked Congress for a declaration of war, saying that the country could no longer tolerate England's "state of war against the United States." Madison asked Congress to quickly put the country on war footing by expanding both the army and the navy.

Madison believed the war would end quickly with an American victory. He ordered three invasions of Canada. First, there was to be an assault from Fort Detroit aimed at destroying British supply lines from Montreal. Madison had no standing army and relied on state militias; however, the governors of northeastern states refused to cooperate. Meanwhile, the British had trained soldiers and allied with American Indians led by Tecumseh. The British attacked Fort Detroit and killed two American officers. Major General William Hull, who, by reports, had been drinking heavily, then surrendered unconditionally. He was later court-martialed for cowardice, but Madison interceded and saved him from execution. Another defeat followed at Queenston Heights when the American commanding general had to deal with mutinous New England troops and was forced to retreat to Albany. At this point, Madison lacked the revenue to fund the war and had to rely on high-interest loans from banks in New York and Philadelphia.

The 1812 presidential election took place under the shadow of war. The British, to this point, had fought a defensive war, so there were no disruptions to the voting. Madison was renominated without opposition. However, a dissident group of Democratic-Republicans nominated New York's lieutenant governor, DeWitt Clinton, to oppose Madison. This group hoped to defeat the sitting president by forming a coalition of those opposed to the war, as well as those who felt Madison had been too slow to respond to the British and northerners who had grown tired and unhappy with Southern control of the White House. Madison won reelection by sweeping the south and carrying Pennsylvania. Clinton won the majority of the northeast and received 89 electoral votes to Madison's 128.

Dismayed by the dismal start to the war, Madison was quick to accept Russia's offer to arbitrate the conflict. He sent a delegation that included Albert Gallatin and future president John Quincy Adams to

Europe to negotiate a peace treaty. During this period, despite the notion that "Britannia Rules the Waves," the United States experienced naval successes. This included a victory in the Battle of Lake Erie, where the United States severely damaged the British supply lines and their ability to reinforce military forces in the western theater of the war.

On land, the Americans were meeting with mixed success. General William Henry Harrison defeated the British and the Tecumseh Confederacy at the Battle of the Thames. The death of Tecumseh in the battle ended any chance of the establishment of a United Indian nation. In 1814, Major General Andrew Jackson secured a victory at the Battle of Horseshoe Bend. Despite these victories, the British continued to repel attempts to invade Canada. At the same time, the British succeeded in capturing Fort Niagara and burned the city of Buffalo.

In August of 1814, a British force landed at the Chesapeake Bay, where they defeated the Americans at the Battle of Bladensburg. Prior to the English capturing Washington, Madison fled into Virginia. The British burned a number of buildings, including the White House. The British next moved to Baltimore, where they were repelled and subsequently left the region in September. In the same month, American forces successfully defeated the British Invasion from Canada. The English people were growing weary of the war, and the country's leaders began looking for a way to end it.

The Treaty of Ghent ended the war on December 24, 1814. Prior to this news reaching Madison, General Jackson's troops won what may have been the most significant American victory at the Battle of New Orleans. With Napoleon's defeat at Waterloo marking the end of the Napoleonic Wars, the seizure of American ships by the French and the English also came to an end. Although the outcome of the War of 1812 was considered a standoff, the end of the conflict enhanced Madison's presidential reputation.

Early in Madison's second term, the country entered what is known as the "Era of Good Feelings." The Federalist Party continued to decline in both influence and popularity. The opposition party held the Hartford Convention, which began on December 15, 1814, and ran until January 5, 1815. As related by Cheney, many Republicans viewed the convention

Grave of James Madison

as a step on the road to secession. Vice President Elbridge Gerry advised Madison to issue a "spirited manifesto" in response. The soon-to-be Governor of Virginia, Wilson Cary Nicholas, urged Madison to send in troops. The results of the convention became known, and while there was no insistence on immediate secession, the convention insisted that the United States government "consent to some arrangement whereby the (New England" states may separately or in concert be empowered to assume upon themselves the defense of their territory" - and allow the states to pay for this by withholding federal tax money. The Federalists had overplayed their hand, as the convention proved to be a burden the party had to carry at a time when Americans had moved toward unity in celebration of what many viewed as a successful "second war of independence" against England.

Madison also contributed to the fall of the Federalists by supporting programs he had previously opposed. He proposed the re-establishment of a national bank and called for a tariff on imported goods. He was successful on both counts, causing strict constructionists such as John Randolph to complain that Madison now "out Hamiltons Alexander Hamilton."

In the 1816 election, both Jefferson and Madison supported James Monroe. Monroe easily defeated the Federalist candidate Rufus King of New York. Madison left office as a very popular president. The former Federalist president John Adams wrote that Madison had "acquired more glory, and established more union, than all of his three predecessors, Washington, Adams and Jefferson, put together."

On June 28, 1836, Madison passed away in his home. He was buried in the family cemetery, but since he had not designed a tombstone, his grave was unmarked. Madison's legacy is a great one. The historian J. C. A. Stagg wrote, "In some ways because he was on the winning side of every important issue facing the young nation from 1776 to 1816 - Madison was the most successful and possibly the most influential of all the Founding Fathers."

Dolley Madison
(1768 – 1849)

The Elegant Hostess

Buried at Madison Family Cemetery at Montpelier,
Montpelier Station, Orange County, Virginia.

Spearhead of Bipartisan Cooperation

She was the wife of the fourth President of the United States. In this role, she was instrumental in defining the role of the President's spouse, later known as the First Lady. She came to the White House with some experience, having served as an unofficial hostess for the widowed Thomas Jefferson during his presidency. Until her husband became President, social gatherings at the White House were typically attended by members of only one political party at a time, as mixing the two parties sometimes resulted in physical altercations and the occasional duel. She demonstrated that members of each party could gather and socialize in a peaceful, bipartisan manner. Her name was Dolley Madison.

Dolley was born as Dolley Payne on May 20, 1768, at Paige's Tavern in Person County, North Carolina. Her parents, John Payne Jr. and Mary Cole, who were married in 1761, hailed from two prominent Virginia families. The couple were Quakers, and in 1769, they decided to return to Virginia. Some historians have speculated that the reason for the move may have been due to local opposition to their religion, a failure in farming, or a combination of both. Eventually, the family, she had three sisters and four brothers, moved back to Cedar Creek, North Carolina, where

Dolley Madison

she experienced a strict Quaker upbringing and education. The historian Richard N. Côté wrote that it was a situation she was "chafing" under.

Dolley's father, John Payne, being a pacifist, did not participate in the American Revolutionary War. By 1783, he had emancipated all his slaves. That same year, he moved the family to Philadelphia. Here, Dolley grew into womanhood, and one of her biographers writes that she was described "as one of the fairest of the fair."

As recounted by Lynne Cheney in her work, *James Madison: A Life Reconsidered*, Payne attempted to support his family by manufacturing laundry starch. The business failed in 1789, which was seen as a weakness by the Quakers, and he was expelled from the Quaker meetings. Devastated and overwhelmed by the turn of events, he took to his bed. Dolley fulfilled her father's dying wish by marrying a promising twenty-seven-year-old Quaker attorney, John Todd. The newly married couple, together with Dolley's sister Anna, moved into a brick house at Fourth and Walnut Streets. Meanwhile, Dolley's mother began to take in borders, one of whom was Aaron Burr.

Dolley and Todd had two sons: John Payne, born in 1792, and William Temple, who entered the world on July 4, 1793. In August of that year, a yellow fever epidemic broke out in Philadelphia. More than 5,000 people died in four months. Dolley lost her husband, her son William and both her father-in-law and mother-in-law.

Dolley's husband had left her money in his will. Now, she was without financial support, and her brother-in-law, who was the executor of the will, was withholding the funds. With the assistance of Aaron Burr, she filed a suit to get what she was owed. In a will written at the time, Burr was also named the guardian of Dolley's surviving son.

James Madison had known Burr since they had both been students at Princeton. So, it was not unusual when he approached Burr to be introduced to the widow Todd. Dolley wrote to a friend, "Aaron Burr says that the great little Madison has asked him to bring him to see me this evening." Congressman Madison was immediately smitten after the meeting. Soon, he confided in Dolley about his feelings through her friend, Catherine Cole. "Now for Madison," Cole wrote on June 1, 1794, "He told me I might say what I pleased to you about him. To begin, he thinks so much of you in the day that he has lost his tongue; at night, he dreams of you and starts in his sleep calling on you to relieve his flame, for he burns to such an excess that he will be shortly consumed, and he hopes that your heart will be callous to every other swain but himself."

Dolley had several other suitors, including a prominent Philadelphia attorney. Madison, however, had quite a bit going for him. He had already reached a level of fame and respect that few in the young nation could match. Not to mention the fact that even greater successes might well be in his future. As told by Cheney, Dolley realized that she would be expelled from meetings if she married outside the Quaker faith but notes she may well have looked to that event with relief.

In August 1794, Dolley wrote to Madison a letter accepting his marriage proposal. On the morning of her wedding, she wrote a letter to a friend saying Madison was "the man whom of all others I most admire." The couple exchanged vows on September 15, 1794. It was a union that would endure for forty-two years until the death of James Madison.

The couple lived in Philadelphia for the next three years. In 1797, rejecting the advice of Jefferson, who urged him to remain in office, Madison decided not to run for reelection. He moved his family back to Montpelier. John Adams wrote to his wife Abigail on Madison's retirement, saying, "It is marvelous how political plants grow in the shade." While Madison had no plans to reenter the political fray, he certainly supported the ambitions of his friend Jefferson. If Jefferson succeeded in gaining the presidency, there was little doubt he would call on Madison to assist him in some capacity. In that event, Madison would, as Adams had said, benefit from time spent out of the political glare.

The Madisons lived in Virginia until 1800, when Jefferson was elected President and picked Madison to serve as his Secretary of State. They moved to Washington into a large house on F Street because, in Dolley's view, space was needed for entertainment, which she believed would be important in the new capital.

They weren't long in Washington before the Madison's began to entertain and in a markedly different way than that of President Jefferson. The President hosted small dinner parties, where the guests were generally all men. In those instances when women were included, he would invite Dolley and her sister Anna to act as hostesses. At first, his dinners were bipartisan, but this ended quickly because he disliked political debates at the table. Soon, he invited only members of one party, and even then, he discouraged discussions of political issues. The Madison's invited both men and women, members of both parties and were fine with political issues being the topic of conversation. As related by Cheney, the Federalist John Quincy Adams wrote in his diary of a party at the Madisons', "There was a company of about seventy persons of both sexes," and he noted that he "had considerable conversation with Mr. Madison on the subjects now most important to the public." People enjoyed the Madisons' parties in large part because of Dolley's considerable and seemingly artless charm. As for the Secretary of State, he dropped his public persona and was warm, friendly and witty. Republicans grew fonder of him, and Federalists soon found it more difficult to demonize him.

After serving two terms, Jefferson, following Washington's lead, announced he would not seek another term. In the 1808 election, it was evident that the Republican nominee would be the next President. Madison had Jefferson's backing and another key advantage with the congressional caucus in naming the Republican nominee. Dolley was skilled at dealing with members of Congress. She repeatedly invited them to her home, where they were welcome to spend hours at a time. In her Madison biography, Cheney notes that Senator Samuel Mitchell, in a letter to his wife, described the edge that Dolley's social gatherings gave Madison over his rival, Vice President George Clinton. "The former gives dinners and makes generous displays to the members. The latter lives smug at his lodgings and keeps aloof from such captivating exhibitions. The secretary of state has a wife to aid his pretensions. The vice president has no female support on his side. And in those two respects, Mr. M is going greatly ahead of him.

Another potential challenger to Madison was James Monroe. Dolley, according to John Quincy Adams, "spoke very slightly of Mr. Monroe." It was easy to understand this when one considers that Monroe was supposed to be her husband's friend, and it was likely that, for the second time, he was being encouraged to run against him. In 1788, Patrick Henry had convinced Monroe to run against Madison, and now Congressman John Randolph of Roanoke was doing the same.

As the election approached, rumors circulated regarding Dolley's morals. Senator Mitchell wrote his wife, "Your friend Mrs. Madison is shockingly and unfeelingly traduced in the Virginia papers." It was clear that one of those encouraging rumors was John Randolph. While Monroe never presented himself as a candidate, he also failed to shut the door on the possibility, saying he would serve if elected. Ultimately, Madison was nominated and subsequently elected as the county's fourth president. He would be reelected in 1812 and serve as the chief executive from 1809 to 1817. Dolley became the official White House hostess, where she was known for her social graces, which contributed to her husband's popularity. She was the only First Lady given an honorary seat on the floor of Congress and the first American to respond to a telegraph message.

In June 1812, during the presidential election campaign, the United States declared war against Great Britain. In 1814, a British force attacked Washington, D.C., following the defeat of inexperienced

Grave of Dolley Madison

American militia forces in the Battle of Bladensburg. As the English force approached and the White House staff prepared to flee, Dolley had her servant, Paul Jennings, save the Stuart painting of George Washington. On August 23, she wrote her sister saying, "Our kind friend Mr. Carroll has come to hasten my departure and in a very bad humor with me, because I insist on waiting until the large picture of General Washington is secured, and it requires to be unscrewed from the wall. The process was found to be too tedious for these perilous moments. I have ordered the frame to be broken and the canvas taken out . . . It is done, and the precious portrait placed in the hands of two gentlemen from New York for safekeeping." At the time, Dolley was credited with removing the painting and portrayed as a national heroine. As it turns out, in an 1865 memoir written by Jennings, he stated that Dolley had ordered him to save the painting and that Jean Pierre Sioussat and a gardener removed it.

Dolley fled Washington in her carriage along with numerous other families. She went to Georgetown and crossed the Potomac into Virginia the following day. The British entered the city and burned the White House and other buildings. When the Madison's returned to the capital, they found the White House to be uninhabitable, so the couple moved into Octagon House.

When Madison left office in 1817, he and Dolley returned to the Montpelier in Virginia. Madison died there at the age of 85 on June 28, 1836. Dolley stayed at the plantation for a year, and her sister Anna and her son John Payne Todd moved in with her. In the fall of 1837, she returned to Washington, leaving Todd to run the plantation. As a result of his alcoholism, he failed. Dolley was forced to sell Montpelier, the remaining slaves, and the furnishings to pay outstanding debts.

Dolley died in Washington in 1849 at the age of 81. She was originally laid to rest in Washington's Congressional Cemetery but was later re-interned at Montpelier next to her husband.

James Monroe
(1758 – 1831)

"The Last Cocked Hat"

Buried at Hollywood Cemetery,
Richmond, Virginia.

———————————

President • Secretary of State • Secretary of War

James Monroe played many roles in the founding of the United States. He was a very busy man who fought bravely in the Continental Army in the Revolutionary War at many key battles and was almost killed at the Battle of Trenton. He was a lawyer and served in the Virginia Legislature, Continental Congress, and United States Senate. He served as Minister to France for George Washington and then Minister to Great Britain for Thomas Jefferson. In between those assignments, he was elected Governor of Virginia and helped secure the Louisiana Purchase. Under President Madison, he served as Secretary of State and Secretary of War and for a while, he was both. Finally, he was elected as our fifth President and served two terms, after which he was elected as a delegate to the Virginia Constitutional Convention and served as the presiding officer until his failing health caused him to withdraw.

———————————

James Monroe was born on April 28, 1758, in his parents' house in Westmoreland County, Virginia. A roadside plaque marks the spot and is listed on the National Registry of Historic Places. He was the second of five children born to Spence and Elizabeth Jones Monroe. Spence was

James Monroe

a prosperous planter of Scottish descent and was involved in protests against the Stamp Act. Little is known about Elizabeth except she was the daughter of a wealthy Welsh immigrant. The family owned 600 acres in Virginia.

At the age of eleven, he enrolled at Campbelltown Academy and took advanced courses in Latin and Math at the College of William and Mary. He became lifetime friends with a classmate and future Chief Justice of the Supreme Court, John Marshall.

By 1774, he had lost both parents and was looked after by his uncle Joseph Jones. Jones was a member of the Virginia House of Burgesses and close friends with George Washington, Thomas Jefferson and James Madison. In 1774, Jones took Monroe to Williamsburg and enrolled him at William and Mary. A year and a half later, the War for Independence erupted, and Monroe dropped out of college and joined the Continental

Army. As he was literate, healthy and a good shot, after months of training, he was ordered to serve in the New York and New Jersey campaigns, and his regiment played an important role in the Army's retreat. In late December 1776, Monroe was with George Washington as he planned and executed the famous attack on Hessian troops at Trenton, New Jersey. Monroe was sent ahead to secure a crossroad leading into Trenton. A local man, Dr. John Riker, when he discovered that the detachment was American, insisted he be allowed to go along, saying he "may be able to help some poor fellow. Monroe finally agreed, and Dr. Riker rode along into the battle. The attack was successful, but Monroe was seriously wounded and nearly died. A bullet grazed the left side of Monroe's chest, then hit his shoulder and injured an artery that bled profusely. His life was saved by Dr. Riker, who stopped the bleeding by sticking his index finger into the wound and applying pressure. Surgeons later attempted to remove the bullet but could not find it. He recovered in eleven weeks but carried the bullet in his shoulder for the rest of his life. George Washington cited Monroe for his bravery and promoted him to Captain. He was eighteen years old.

After recovering, Monroe asked to be returned to the front and was at the Battle of Brandywine, where he formed a close friendship with the Marquis de Lafayette. He went on to serve in the Philadelphia campaign and spent the winter of 1777–78 at Valley Forge, sharing a hut with John Marshall. In late 1777, he was promoted to Major. After serving as a scout at the Battle of Monmouth, he resigned from the Army and began to study law at William and Mary under Thomas Jefferson, who was then Governor of Virginia. Through Thomas Jefferson, Monroe formed a friendship with James Madison. He was elected to the Virginia assembly in 1782 and to the Continental Congress in 1783 at the age of twenty-five. While in New York serving in Congress, he met Elizabeth Kortright, and they married at Trinity Church in Manhattan on February 16, 1786. She was seventeen, and he was twenty-seven. The couple would have three children.

In the fall of that year, Monroe resigned from Congress, moved to Fredericksburg, Virginia, and became an attorney for the state. The next year, he was elected again to the Virginia House of Delegates and in 1788, he became a delegate to the Virginia Ratifying Convention. The Ratifying Convention ratified the Constitution, but Monroe voted against it. He opposed the Electoral College and wanted the direct election of Senators and a strong Bill of Rights. After the Constitution was ratified, Monroe challenged James Madison for a seat in the House of Representatives. Monroe lost by 300 votes, and the two became close friends. In a twist of fate, when Senator William Grayson died in 1790 while serving in the Senate, John Walker was appointed to serve from March 31 to November 9, when Monroe was elected to replace him.

While in the Senate, Monroe was on a committee to investigate charges of financial malfeasance against Alexander Hamilton. When interviewing Hamilton, he revealed that the transactions in question were hush money to keep Hamilton's affair with James Reynolds' wife secret. Word got to the press, and Hamilton blamed Monroe for the leak. It almost led to a duel, but ironically none other than Aaron Burr stepped in and defused the tension. It was the nation's first political sex scandal.

In 1794 Washington appointed Monroe as his Minister to France. Monroe's tenure in France was far from easy. France was an unstable place, and Monroe had to be careful. His mission was to uphold Washington's policy of neutrality between France and Britain. He had early success, but the Jay Treaty with Britain caused relations with France to deteriorate. Monroe was blamed, and with Hamilton's urging, Monroe was recalled in November 1796. He returned to Virginia to practice law and tend to his plantations. He was elected governor in 1799 and worked vigorously in support of Thomas Jefferson for President in 1800. He served as governor until 1802 and then was appointed as a special envoy to help negotiate the Louisiana Purchase.

Monroe then served as the United States Minister to Britain from 1803 to 1807. During this time, Jefferson offered him the position of First Governor of Louisiana Territory, but Monroe turned it down and remained Minister to Britain. His main assignment was to negotiate an end to the impressment of US sailors. Jefferson sent William Pinkney to London to assist Monroe. The two negotiated a treaty with Britain that contained no provision against impressment. Jefferson was upset that they disregarded their instructions and refused to submit the treaty to the Senate for ratification. This caused a rift in Monroe's relationship with Jefferson and James Madison, the Secretary of State.

Monroe returned home in 1807 and ran for President against James Madison in the 1808 election. Madison won big, and afterward, the two reconciled. In 1810, Monroe returned to the Virginia House of Delegates and, in 1811, was again elected Governor, though he did not serve for long. That April, Madison named him Secretary of State. The Senate unanimously confirmed him 30–0. He was unable to make progress with Britain on attacking American merchant ships and impressment of US sailors to serve on British war ships against France. Thus, Madison asked Congress to declare War on Britain, and Congress did so on June 18, 1812.

The War went badly, and in August 1814, British troops and warships appeared at the mouth of the Potomac. Monroe personally scouted the Chesapeake Bay and, on August 21, sent the President a warning so that he and his wife could flee. The British burned the Capitol and the White House on August 24. Madison removed John Armstrong as Secretary of War and appointed Monroe on September 27. No successor was appointed at State, and thus Monroe held both posts from October 1814 to February 28, 1815. The Treaty of Ghent ended the war in February 1815. Monroe resigned as Secretary of War in March and returned to State, his popularity soaring. In 1816, Monroe was elected President, defeating Rufus King, the Federalist candidate. He was the last founder to serve as President. He received 183 electoral votes to 34 for King. He was reelected in 1820, receiving all electoral votes but one. He had a calm, peaceful, prosperous administration, which has been called the Era of Good Feelings.

He ignored old party lines in making appointments and appointed a geographically balanced cabinet including John Quincy Adams as Secretary of State. The main events of his administration were the acquisition of Florida from Spain via the Adams-Oni Treaty, the Missouri Compromise, which temporarily settled the slavery issue in the territories, recognition of former Spanish colonies in Central and South America (Argentina, Peru, Columbia, Chile and Mexico), and the Monroe Doctrine in which Monroe warns European nations that the US would not tolerate further colonization or puppet monarchs in the Western Hemisphere.

James Monroe's crypt

Throughout his tenure, Monroe was the last president to wear a pow-dered wig tied in a queue, a tricorn hat, and knee-breeches as was cus-tomary in the late 1700s, earning him the nickname "The Last Cocked Hat." At the end of his second term, Monroe retired to his home, an estate called Oak Hill in northern Virginia, now included in the grounds of the University of Virginia. He began working on an autobiography but died before it could be completed. It was published in 1959 and is still available. He was plagued by money problems in retirement and sold his Highland Plantation, which is now owned by the College of William and Mary and is open to the public as a historic site.

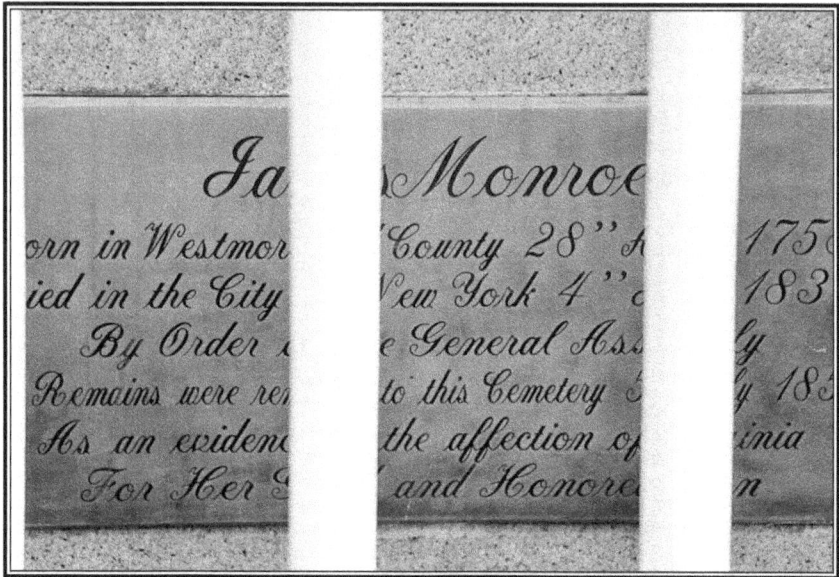

Monroe's grave

In 1829, Monroe was elected as a delegate to the Virginia Constitutional Convention and elected by the convention to be the presiding officer. He withdrew after two months due to health concerns. He moved to New York in 1830 to live with his daughter Maria. His wife had died a year before. He died there in 1831 at the age of 73 on July 4, thus becoming the third president on Independence Day. Thomas Jefferson and John Adams both died on Independence Day, five years before him. He was originally buried in the New York City Marble Cemetery. In 1858, the centennial year of his birth, his remains were reinterred at the Presidents Circle in Hollywood Cemetery in Richmond, Virginia. The James Monroe Tomb is a United States National Historic Landmark. After Liberia was created in 1821 as a haven for freed slaves, its capital city was named Monrovia in his honor. He had supported the repatriation of black people to Africa.

James Monroe was the last president not photographed in his lifetime. His successor, John Quincy Adams, was the first.

Thomas Adams
(1730–1788)

Delegate from Virginia

Body lost or destroyed / burial site unknown.

———•◦•———

Articles of Confederation

Some of the founders of our country are well known to almost all Americans. Others we become aware of through American History courses. Still, others are known to only serious students of United States history. There are a few founders whose memory has been lost to all but those who have examined the revolutionary period under a microscope. This founder falls into the latter category. When one sees or hears the name Adams associated with the founding of the United States, thoughts immediately are drawn to the state of Massachusetts and Samuel, John, and Abigail. This founder was not even a relative of that trio, and he hailed from Virginia. His name was Thomas Adams, and he served in the Continental Congress during the American Revolution, where he added his signature to the Articles of Confederation.

———◆◦◆———

Adams was born sometime in 1730 in New Kent County, Virginia. His grandfather was a tailor and has been described as one of London's leading merchants. He was educated at what was known as the common school, which was a reference to nonurban institutions of learning. It is unknown if he attended any institutions of higher learning, but whatever education he did receive qualified him to work as the clerk of Henrico County, Virginia.

Thomas Adams

According to his Congressional biography, from 1762 until 1774, Adams lived in England, where he had extensive business interests. When he returned to America, tensions between the mother country and the colonies were high. He sided with his fellow colonists in opposing the harsh economic policies adopted by the English Parliament. Shortly after returning to the country of his birth, he was elected to the Virginia House of Burgesses. He was among the delegates who signed the Articles of Association. This document strongly criticized the British government and its "ruinous system of colony administration." The Articles, in Virginia, were the result of the action taken by the colonial governor, John Murray, when he dissolved the House of Burgesses. It was at this time that Adams became chairman of the New Kent County Committee of Safety.

In 1778 Adams was elected to represent Virginia in the Continental Congress. He would serve in the Congress for two years, and it was in this capacity that he affixed his signature to the Articles of Confederation.

In 1780 Adams left the Congress and moved to Augusta County, Virginia. He was elected to the Virginia State Senate, where he served from 1783 until 1786. After retiring from public service, he lived the remainder of his days on his estate known as the "Cowpasture." It was here he passed away on July 8, 1788. Very little detail exists relative to this Founder's life. Almost none of his letters have survived. The College of William and Mary has nine letters that involve Adams though most deal with his family's burial ground. The location of his burial site is unknown.

Even with so little information left behind, it is possible to surmise the qualities that Adams possessed. His business success suggests that he was intelligent and industrious. The faith his fellow citizens had in him is attested to by the many positions he held as an elected representative. His courage is evident because he supported the revolution against England even though he had significant business interests in the mother country. In short, his character was in keeping with the many well and better-known founders who were his contemporaries.

John Banister
(1734–1788)

The Master of Hatcher's Run

Buried at Hatcher's Run Estate,
Dinwiddie County, Virginia.

Articles of Confederation

Colonel John Banister was an attorney and plantation owner from Petersburg, Virginia. He served in the Virginia House of Burgesses and as an officer in the Virginia Militia. He was elected to the Second Continental Congress, where he signed the Articles of Confederation.

Banister, born December 26, 1734, at the family's estate, Hatcher's Run, near Petersburg, Dinwiddie County, Virginia, was the son of Captain John Banister, a ship's captain, and his wife, Martha Wilmette (née Munford) Banister. Banister's grandfather, John Baptist Banister (1654–1692), was one of the first university-trained naturalists in North America, referred to as "the first Virginia botanist of any note."

Young Banister traveled on his father's ship, crossing the Atlantic to England, where he attended Wakefield, a private school south of Leeds. He then studied law at the Temple Inn in London, admitted on September 27, 1753. Upon graduation, Banister was admitted to the Virginia bar and opened a law practice in Petersburg. He also managed his plantation.

Banister married Elizabeth Munford in 1755. He was first elected to the Virginia House of Burgesses in 1765 and served until 1769. During

COL. JOHN BANISTER.

John Banister

this time, he and Elizabeth built a suburban villa in Petersburg called Battersea. It was in the five-part Palladian style and completed in 1768. John Banister Jr., known as Jack, was born to this couple, though the exact year is not recorded. Likewise, a daughter, Maria Ann, was born, though the date is lost. She later married the physician George Wilson from Petersburg. Unfortunately, Elizabeth died in 1770.

Banister next married Elizabeth "Patsy" Bland, the daughter of Theodorick Bland of Cawsons, a descendant of one of Virginia's first families, and a son of Continental Congressman Richard Bland. She was also the sister of Colonel Theodorick Bland, who later became a Continental Congressman and member of the First Congress. The couple gave birth to son Robert Bannister in 1771, but he lived only until 1794.

Banister returned to the House of Burgesses in 1772 until 1775, when his wife died that year.

Home of John Banister

As tensions rose with England, Banister was a member of the Virginia Convention, which declared Virginia independent in 1776. He was elected to the new Virginia House of Delegates in 1776 and served until 1778.

On November 19, 1777, Banister was elected to the Second Continental Congress, which met in York, Pennsylvania. There, he was one of the framers of the Articles of Confederation, which he signed on July 8, 1778.

Banister next joined the Virginia Militia as a cavalry officer in 1778 at the major, rising to the rank of lieutenant colonel by 1781. During this time, Banister became good friends with Thomas Jefferson.

In 1779, Banister married Agan Blair of Williamsburg, Virginia, the daughter of John Blair Sr., a nephew of James Blair, the founder of William and Mary College, and the father of John Blair Jr., who signed the Constitution. John Blair Sr. was a longtime member of the House of Burgesses and acting governor. The couple had sons Burrell Banister (1779–1837) and Theodorick Blair Banister (1780–1829) early in their marriage.

During the weeks before the Battle of Yorktown in 1781, Lieutenant Colonel Banister, highly regarded by George Washington, aided in supplying and repelling the British army from Virginia. In so doing, he lost most of his personal property to the British led by General William Phillips, who often stayed at Battersea and confiscated his valuables.

Sign pointing the way to John Banister's estate, Battersea.

After the war, Banister returned to the House of Delegates from 1781 until 1784. By 1782, he appears to have recovered his assets, as Dinwiddie County records note: three free males, 46 adult slaves, 42 underage slaves, 28 horses, 126 cattle, and one chariot. He and Agan had another son, John Monro Banister (1784–1832). Also, in 1784, son "Jack" accompanied Thomas Jefferson to France.

In 1785, Banister was appointed the first mayor of Petersburg and was noted for his knowledge of current affairs and his writing accomplishments.

Banister died on September 30, 1788, at Hatcher's Run, three months short of his 54th birthday. He was buried in the family plot there. His eldest son, "Jack" Banister, died eleven weeks later, owing Thomas Jefferson 3173 livres following his time in Europe. This great debt may have greatly impacted the Banisters, leading to small or no inheritances for the minor children, Burrell and Monro.

Daughter Maria Ann Wilson died in October 1792. Ann Blair Banister died on December 23, 1813.

John Blair Jr.
(1732 – 1800)

Grand Master of Virginia

Buried at Bruton Parish Churchyard,
Williamsburg, Virginia.

————•◦•————

US Constitution • US Supreme Court

John Blair, Jr., was a lawyer from Williamsburg, Virginia, whose family
had close ties to the College of William and Mary and the colonial government. Blair represented Virginia at the US Constitutional Convention
and signed the resulting document. He was then appointed one of the
first Associate Justices of the US Supreme Court.

————◦◦◦————

Blair was born in Williamsburg, Virginia, on April 17, 1732. He
was one of twelve children of John Blair, a member of the Virginia
House of Burgesses, and his wife, Mary (née Monro), the granddaugh-
ter of Reverend John Monro of St. John's Parish, King William County,
Virginia. The elder Blair served in the Virginia colonial government as
a burgess, on the Governor's Council, and as acting Royal Governor
on four occasions. Dr. Archibald Blair, the paternal grandfather, was
also a member of the House of Burgesses. His brother, Reverend James
Blair, was the founder and president of the College of William and
Mary. Upon Reverend James's passing, John Senior inherited most of
the estate.

Both father and son were graduates of the College of William and
Mary. Young John completed his degree in 1754. He then went to

John Blair Jr. (1732–1800)

John Blair, Jr.

London to study law at the Middle Temple in 1755. Blair married his cousin, Jean Balfour (1736–1792) in Edinburgh, Scotland, while visiting in 1756. The couple had two children. Blair was admitted to the Virginia bar in 1757.

One of Blair's first assignments was an appointment as representative in the House of Burgesses for the College of William and Mary at a time when his father was on the Governor's Council. Blair served in this capacity from 1766 to 1799. He also served other roles in the colonial government through 1780.

Blair became involved in the patriot cause in Virginia, joining George Washington and others in 1770 and 1774 in the declaration of nonimportation agreements in response to unjust taxes imposed by the British Parliament. Blair also joined in supporting the people of Boston in 1775 following the Intolerable Acts.

In 1776, Blair helped to prepare the Virginia Declaration of Rights and the new Virginia Constitution. During the American Revolution, Blair served as a judge in several state courts and was a highly respected jurist, staying out of public political debates. He also served on Governor Patrick Henry's Privy Council of advisors from 1776 to 1778. In 1782, as a judge on the Virginia Court of Appeals, Blair ruled that courts could declare legislative acts unconstitutional. The case, *The Commonwealth of Virginia v. Caton el al* helped set precedence for the US Supreme Court's later case, *Marbury v. Madison.*

Throughout his life, Blair was a devout Freemason. He was a Master of the Williamsburg Lodge and organized the formation of the Grand Lodge of Virginia in 1777. Blair was elected the Grand Master of the Virginia Lodge on October 13, 1778.

As an adherent of James Madison and proponent of national union, Blair joined the Constitutional Convention of 1787, but there is no account of his speaking or serving on any committees. He signed the document with quiet approval. He then pushed for its ratification by Virginia.

On September 24, 1789, President George Washington nominated Blair to the US Supreme Court as one of the five associate justices serving with Chief Justice John Jay. He had sought "the first characters of the Union" for the body. Blair wrote in response to Washington, "When I considered the great importance, as well as the arduous nature of the duties, I could not but entertain some fears." Nevertheless, he "determined to make an experiment, whether I may be able to perform the requisite services, with some degree of satisfaction, in respect both to the Public and my self."

The Senate confirmed him two days later, and Blair served until October 25, 1795, when he resigned. Only thirteen cases were decided by the court over those first six years. Blair was a proponent of the supremacy of the Constitution, where appropriate, in all matters legal in the new country. Blair wrote regarding one decision, "The constitution of the United States is the only fountain from which I shall draw; the only authority to which I shall appeal."

James Sullivan, attorney general of Massachusetts, wrote to United States Senator William Bingham, "I think the President has been very fortunate in the appointment of Judges. We are much pleased with Judge

Grave of John Blair

Blair who has been with us. His candor ease politeness and learning are acknowledged and I am no less pleased with his independence."

Blair's resignation was due to health reasons. At the time of his resignation, he wrote the president. "A strange disorder of my head, which has lately compel'd me to neglect my official duties, . . . has for some time past made me contemplate the resignation of my office, as an event highly probable . . . I return you now the commission by which I have been so highly honoured."

Upon learning of Blair's retirement, Senator William Plumer from New Hampshire wrote, "I consider him as a man of good abilities, not indeed a Jay, but far superior to Cushing, a man of firmness, strict integrity and of great candour."

After Jean's death in 1792, Blair became a widower and returned to Williamsburg following his resignation, spending the rest of his life there. In 1797, Blair wrote to his sister about another health episode, "I happened to be employed in some algebraical exercises . . . when all at once a torpid numbness seized my whole face and I found my intellectual powers much weakened, and all was confusion. My tongue partook of the distress, and some words I was not able to articulate distinctly, and a general difficulty of remembering words at all."

Blair passed away on August 31, 1800, and is buried in the churchyard of Bruton Parish Church in Williamsburg. He was 68 years old.

Blair Street in Madison, Wisconsin, was named in his honor. John Blair House remains in the town of Williamsburg as a historic site, part of which was the original house of James Blair.

Richard Bland
(1710 – 1776)

Planter and Pamphleteer

Buried at Jordan Point Plantation, on the Jordan Point Manor,
Prince George County, Virginia.

———————

Continental Association • Continental Congress

———————

Richard Bland was a wealthy plantation owner from Prince George
County, Virginia, who was orphaned at a young age. Raised by his
aunts and uncles, Bland was very close to cousins Peyton Randolph
and Thomas Jefferson via his late mother's Randolph line. Bland was a
longtime member of the Virginia House of Burgesses who was an early
patriot, challenging the right of the British Parliament to impose taxes.
Bland was elected to the First Continental Congress, where he was one of
the oldest members. He signed the Continental Association.

———————

Bland was born May 6, 1710, at either Jordan's Point Plantation
in Prince George County, Virginia, or Bland House in Williamsburg,
Virginia. He was the oldest son of Richard Bland, a wealthy planter,
and his second wife, Elizabeth (née Randolph), a sister of Richard and
William Randolph. The elder Bland owned a thousand-acre plantation
along the James River, about sixty-five miles north of the Chesapeake
Bay. Both parents were from old Virginia families.

In 1720, during Richard's tenth year, his mother died on January 22
and his father on April 6. Richard and his four siblings were orphaned

Richard Bland

and raised by their uncles, William and Richard Randolph. These men acted as guardians, looked after the plantation, and raised and educated the children. During this time, Richard became very close to his first cousin, Peyton Randolph, a relationship that would last throughout his life.

The heir to an incredible estate, Blair was educated at the College of William and Mary and Edinburgh University in Scotland. He studied law, though he never practiced in court as an attorney. He was admitted to the Virginia bar in 1746.

Bland was married three times: first to Anne Poythress in 1730 until her death in 1758; for only eight months in 1759 to Martha Massie, a widow who passed away that same year; and lastly in 1760 to Elizabeth Blair Bolling, until her death in 1775. Richard and Anne had twelve children, including six sons and six daughters.

Bland first served as a justice of the peace in Prince George County. He was made a militia officer in 1739 and was often referred to as "Colonel" Bland in later years. Bland was elected to the Virginia House of Burgesses in 1742, serving 33 years until 1775. He wrote several pamphlets over these years pertaining to the clergy and to colonial government.

In 1766, in response to the Sugar Act of 1764 and the Stamp Act of 1765, he penned the pamphlet *An Inquiry into the Rights of the British Colonies*, questioning Parliament's right to impose taxes on the colonies. Wrote Bland:

> The Question is whether the Colonies are represented in the British Parliament or not? You affirm it to be an indubitable Fact that they are represented, and from thence you infer a Right in the Parliament to impose Taxes of every Kind upon them. You do not insist upon the Power, but upon the Right of Parliament to impose Taxes upon the Colonies. This is certainly a very proper Distinction, as Right and Power have very different Meanings, and convey very different Ideas; For had you told us that the Parliament of Great Britain have Power, by the Fleets and Armies of the Kingdom, to impose Taxes and to raise Contributions upon the Colonies, I should not have presumed to dispute the Point with you; but as you insist upon the Right only, I must beg Leave to differ from you in Opinion, and shall give my Reasons for it.

Around this same time, James Otis, Jr. made similar arguments in Massachusetts. John Adams later paraphrased Otis, summarizing the protest as "Taxation without Representation is Tyranny." Bland, Otis, and others made similar arguments for this ancient concept, harkening back to chapter 12 of the *Magna Carta*, "(n)o scutage or aid is to be levied in our kingdom, save by the common counsel of our kingdom."

As tensions increased with the British, Bland was appointed to Virginia's Committee of Correspondence in 1773. In response to a call for a Continental Congress to convene in Philadelphia in October 1774, Bland was elected on August 5, though he still hoped for reconciliation with Britain. He then traveled to Philadelphia with his fellow Virginia delegates. Bland attended what became known as the First Continental Congress in October 1774. John Adams described Bland as a "learned, bookish man" in his diary. Concepts from Bland's pamphlet made it into Congress's Declaration of Rights on October 14, 1774. The Congress then signed the Continental Association on October 20, 1774.

Following the Battles of Lexington and Concord, Bland returned for the May 1775 session of Congress but declined to accept the appointment to another term on account of his health. Instead, he returned to Virginia with Peyton Randolph, now convinced the path to independence was necessary. There, he joined an eleven-man Committee of Safety that governed the colony following the collapse of the royal government. Bland also attended the Virginia Convention from December 1775 to June 1776, determined to establish a new constitution for the colony.

Grave of Richard Bland

Bland next returned to Williamsburg, and soon after, on October 26, 1776, he collapsed in the street. He was removed to the house of John Tazewell, a friend, where he died later that night at the age of 66. Bland was buried on the Jordan Point Plantation, on the Jordan Point Manor, next to his father and other relatives. His tombstone reads, "In Memory, Richard Bland, 1710–1776. *Sperate, Fortes, Et Virite.*" A nearby plaque describes him "as [a] political pamphleteer, constitutional historian, scholar, attorney and public servant [who] championed public rights and represented Virginia in the First and Second Continental Congresses and in all five of Virginia's Revolutionary Conventions."

Bland is further described in the *Dictionary of Virginia Biography*: "[He] was a Virginia planter and statesman whose prolific writings on the colonial right to self-governance helped shape Virginia political opinion in the years leading up to the American Revolution."

Richard Bland College, the junior college of the College of William and Mary, and Bland County in Virginia are named in his honor.

Much of Bland's library was acquired by Thomas Jefferson, who later donated it to the Library of Congress in 1815. Thomas Jefferson remembered his cousin when writing to Thomas Leiper that year:

> Your characters are inimitably and justly drawn. I am not certain if more might not be said of Colonel Richard Bland. He was the most learned and logical man of those who took prominent lead in public affairs, profound in constitutional lore, a most ungraceful speaker . . . He would set out on sound principles, pursue them logically till he found them leading to the recipice [*sic*] which he had to leap, start back alarmed, then resume his ground, go over it in another direction, be led again by the correctness of his reasoning to the same place, and again back about, and try other processes to reconcile right and wrong, but finally left his reader and himself bewildered between the steady index of the compass in their hand, and the phantasm to which it seemed to point. Still there was more sound matter in his pamphlet than in the celebrated Farmer's letters which were really but an *ignis fatuus*, misleading us from true principles.

Daniel Boone

(1734–1820)

Western Pioneer

Original burial site: Daniel Boone Burial Site and Monument,
Marthasville, Missouri.
Reinterred at Frankfort Cemetery,
Frankfort, Kentucky.

———— ◆ ————

Military • Westward Expansion

Daniel Boone was best known for blazing the path through the
Cumberland Gap into Virginia's western claims that became Kentucky.
As an explorer and frontiersman, he was a catalyst for westward expansion, becoming one of the country's first legendary folk heroes. He
founded Boonesborough, one of the first English-speaking settlements
west of the Appalachian Mountains. Over 200,000 settlers followed his
Wilderness Road into Kentucky by the end of the 1700s. During the
American Revolution, Boone was an officer in the militia, leading the
settlers against the British-allied natives. After the Revolution, he worked
as a surveyor and merchant and speculated in land, ultimately moving to
Missouri, west of the Mississippi River.

————— ◆ —————

   Daniel Boone was born on October 22, 1734, in a one-room log
cabin in the Oley Valley of what is now Berks County, Pennsylvania,
to Squire Boone, a weaver and blacksmith, and his wife, Sarah Morgan
Boone. Both of Boone's parents were Quakers. Squire Boone emigrated
from England in 1713. He married Sarah Morgan, whose parents were
Welsh emigrants, in 1720. Daniel was the sixth of eleven children.

Daniel Boone

Young Daniel roamed the wilderness of what was then Lancaster County, about fifty miles west of Philadelphia. He developed a reputation as a superb hunter. One of the tales from these days, likely a folktale, described Boone calmly shooting a mountain lion through the heart with his flintlock musket as the animal was leaping on him.

In 1742, sister Sarah Boone caused a controversy among the Quakers by marrying outside the denomination. Squire and Sarah apologized for this and the fact their daughter was already pregnant. Five years later, when brother Israel also married a non-Quaker, Squire stood by his son, and the two were expelled from the congregation. Sarah continued to attend the meeting house with her children.

Circa 1750, likely fed up with the falling out with the Quakers, Squire Boone sold his land and moved the family to North Carolina, settling on the Yadkin River, west of Mocksville, in what is now Davie County. Daniel Boone did not attend church again for the rest of his life, though he considered himself a Christian and later had his children baptized. He also received little formal education, though family members tutored him. According to family lore, when a schoolteacher asked about Daniel, Squire said, Let the girls do the spelling, and Dan will do the shooting." However, the image of Boone being semiliterate is incorrect. He was known to take the Bible and novels with him while traveling and was often the only literate person in the groups with which he traveled.

Barely twenty when the French and Indian War began, Boone joined the North Carolina militia as a teamster and blacksmith, accompanying General Edward Braddock on his ill-fated mission. It is interesting to note that George Washington, Daniel Boone, Charles Scott, and Horatio Gates were all part of this expedition and survived. Fortunately, Boone was in the rear with his wagon when the devastating attack occurred.

Upon his return to North Carolina, Boone married Rebecca Bryan on August 14, 1756. They lived in a cabin on Squire Boone's farm and eventually had ten children and raised eight more from deceased relatives. War then came to their valley when the Cherokees raided during the Cherokee Uprising in 1758. Boone returned to duty in the militia until 1760. The family, meanwhile, moved north to Culpepper, Virginia.

Following his military service, Boone made a living as a hunter and trapper, harvesting pelts for the fur trade. He and his companions would comb the wilderness for weeks at a time. Often, he would travel alone. One likely apocryphal tale mentioned Boone returning home to find his wife had given birth to a daughter fathered by his brother. They had feared Boone was dead because he did not return when expected. Boone then raised the daughter as his own and forgave his wife. Early biographers omitted this story, but there are conflicting accounts regarding which daughter and which brother.

As the game population decreased in the mid-1760s, Boone found it harder to make a living and was in debt. He attempted a move to Florida, but Rebecca refused to go. Instead, the family moved west of the Blue Ridge Mountains, where the fur trade was still sustainable.

Boone and his brother Squire first set foot in Kentucky in 1767 but failed to find the hunting grounds they were seeking. In 1769, Boone and five companions went on a two-year expedition to explore Kentucky. All did not go well. In late December, Boone and one of his fellow hunters were captured by the Shawnees and robbed of their furs. They were told to never return to what they perceived as their hunting grounds. Upon release, Boone continued his expedition and shot an Indian to escape capture. He returned home in 1771 but was back in Kentucky in 1772.

In 1773, Boone, his brother Squire, and fifty others, attempted to create the first English settlement in Kentucky. William Russell, the brother-in-law of Patrick Henry, was in the group. While foraging, Boone's son, James, and Russell's son, Henry, were tortured and killed by Indians. Boone's party abandoned the expedition and returned home. These events were part of Dunmore's War between Virginia and the natives. Boone assisted as a member of the militia and was promoted to captain. The war ended in October 1774 at the Battle of Point Pleasant. Kentucky was no longer beholden to the Shawnees.

Boone was next hired by a North Carolina judge named Richard Henderson to help establish a colony in this region. He traveled to Cherokee towns to gather a meeting at Sycamore Shoals in March 1775. There, Henderson purchased the Cherokee's claim to Kentucky. Boone then blazed the trail through the Cumberland Gap into central Kentucky called Boone's Trace, later the Wilderness Road. Boone founded Boonesborough in Kentucky, along the Kentucky River. Boone's family joined him on September 8, 1775. This was the first permanent settlement west of the thirteen colonies. Rebecca Boone was the first white woman in the west who was not a captive of the Indians. Kentucky did not immediately become the fourteenth colony. Rather, the settlement was in a western county of Virginia. Boone described a happy life as "a good gun, a good horse, and a good wife."

At the outset of the American Revolution, the natives seized the chance to drive the settlers out of the region. Many left, and only two hundred remained in Kentucky, primarily at the stockaded settlements at Boonesborough, Harrodsburg, and Logan's Station. On July 14, 1776, Boone's daughter and two other girls were captured by the Indians and taken north into the Ohio country. Boone and his men went in pursuit and ambushed the natives, rescuing the girls. This was perhaps the most famous event in Boone's life, fictionalized by James Fenimore Cooper in *The Last of the Mohicans*, published in 1826.

In 1777, the British encouraged native war parties to raid in Kentucky. Early in 1778, Boone and his companions were captured by warriors of Chief Blackfish. Boone then bluffed for time to vacate Boonesborough in the spring since the women and children were unlikely to survive winter in the wilderness. Some of his men did not realize his ruse and thought he had switched sides. This later led to a court-martial of Boone.

Boone and his men were then taken captive to Blackfish's town of Chillicothe. As was their custom, the Shawnees adopted the captives as replacements for fallen warriors. Boone was given the name Sheltowee (Big Turtle) and likely adopted by Blackfish. He accompanied Blackfish to Detroit to meet with British Governor Hamilton, who attempted to sway Boone to switch sides. Boone insisted he would abandon Boonesborough. After returning to Chillicothe on June 16, 1778, Boone learned Blackfish intended to move on Boonesborough. He took off on horseback and then on foot to reach Boonesborough 160 miles away, covering the distance through the wilderness in five days. There he warned the settlers of the pending attack.

Boone led a preemptive attack on the Shawnees to remove any doubt of his loyalty and then successfully defended Boonesborough during Blackfish's siege, which began on September 7, 1778. Following the ten-day siege, Boone was court-martialed but acquitted based on his testimony. He then returned to North Carolina to rejoin his family.

In late 1779, Boone and a large party headed back into Kentucky to find a new settlement called Boone's Station. Among the pioneers was the family of Captain Abraham Lincoln, the grandfather of the future president. Lincoln had also been born in Berks County, a few miles from Boone. When the settlers needed to file land claims in Williamsburg, Virginia, Boone collected over $20,000 from them and returned to Williamsburg to handle the matters on their behalf. While sleeping in a tavern, the cash was stolen. While some settlers forgave Boone for the loss, he worked many years to repay the others.

By the end of the Revolution, Boone was less of a woodsman and more a leading citizen. Boone joined General George Rogers Clark in his invasion of the Ohio country. Following the Battle of Piqua on August 7, 1780, Boone was hunting on his way home with his brother Ned. Shawnees ambushed them, and Ned was killed. The natives believed Ned was Daniel because he resembled him. They removed his head and returned to declare Daniel Boone dead. Meanwhile, Boone returned home and was promoted to lieutenant colonel in November.

The following spring, Boone was elected as the representative to the Virginia Assembly in Richmond. While on the way to take his seat, British dragoons under Banastre Tarleton captured him and several other legislators. The captives were released on parole several days later. The British surrendered at Yorktown in October 1781, but the fighting continued in Kentucky. At the Battle of Blue Licks, in August 1782, Boone's son Israel was killed, and the Kentuckians were defeated. Boone then joined Clark's expedition into Ohio, marking the end of the war. He was then elected sheriff of Fayette County in 1782.

Boone next moved to Limestone (later Maysville), Kentucky, where he kept a tavern and traded horses, speculated in land, and surveyed. In 1784, John Filson's book *The Discovery, Settlement and Present State of Kentucke* was published, which included an account of Boone, making him a celebrity.

The war with the natives heated up again in September 1786. Boone participated in the expedition led by Benjamin Logan. Boone was able to help negotiate a truce and prisoner exchange. However, the hostilities continued until the Battle of Fallen Timbers eight years later.

Over the next decade, Boone attempted numerous business pursuits and moved to several times, including Point Pleasant, now in West Virginia. Unfortunately, he could not maintain his prosperity and was always going into debt. When times were tough, he would give up the trades and go back into the woods to hunt and trap. In the mid-1790s, Boone moved back to Kentucky. In 1798, Boone County was erected and named after him.

In 1799, Boone sought new opportunities outside the United States, traveling to Spanish Louisiana, to what is now St. Charles County, Missouri. There, the Spanish governor appointed Boone judge and military leader in exchange for encouraging settlement. Boone served in this capacity until the Louisiana Purchase was implemented in 1804. Once again, Boone met with financial trouble as his Spanish land grants were now invalid. These claims were not restored until 1814. It is rumored after his lands were restored, Boone made one last trip to Kentucky to pay off his debts, but this is likely a legend.

During his final years in Missouri, despite being in his 70s, Boone accompanied expeditions up the Missouri River as far the Yellowstone River, a round trip of over 2000 miles. In 1816, after reaching Fort Osage on another expedition, an officer wrote of Boone, "We have been honored by a visit from Col. Boone . . . He has taken part in all the wars of America, from Braddock's war to the present hour," but "he prefers the woods, where you see him in the dress of the roughest, poorest hunter."

On September 26, 1820, Daniel Boone died at his son's home on Femme Osage Creek, near Marthasville, Missouri. He was buried next to Rebecca, who had died seven years earlier. The graves were unmarked until the 1830s. In 1845, Boone's remains were disinterred and reburied at the cemetery in Frankfort, Kentucky, by Boone relatives. However, it has been claimed by resentful Missourians that the wrong bodies were dug up and moved because the grave markers were in the wrong place. An examination of a plaster cast of Boone's skull made during the reburial was examined by a forensic anthropologist in 1983 and determined to likely be of an African, most likely a slave buried in the same cemetery. To this day, both locations claim to have the remains of Daniel Boone.

Daniel Boone was a legend in his own time, though many of the stories about him were exaggerations or outright fabrications. Said Boone, "Many heroic actions and chivalrous adventures are related of me which exist only in the regions of fancy. With me, the world has taken great liberties, and yet I have been but a common man."

As mentioned previously, Filson's book of 1784 laid the groundwork for Boone's legend. Most of the accounts in this book are true and were meant to attract settlers to Kentucky. This book was translated into German and French and reprinted numerous times.

In 1822, Lord Byron mentioned Boone in his epic poem, *Don Juan*, likening him to someone who always sought to escape civilization as it began in encroach.

The Biographical Memoir of Daniel Boone, the First Settler of Kentucky, was based on an interview of Boone by Timothy Flint. This book was

Daniel Boone's memorial in Frankfurt, Kentucky.

published in 1833 and became one of the best-selling biographies of the century. Like Parson Weems's treatment of George Washington, Flint embellished Boone's adventures, including fighting with bears and swinging from vines. The family was embarrassed by these exaggerations, but they were popular with boys and were often the subject of dime novels.

Over the years, Boone's legend grew. In 1852, Henry Tuckerman dubbed him "the Columbus of the woods." Later, historian Michael Lofaro called Boone "the founding father of westward expansion." During the latter part of the 1800s, Boone was portrayed as an Indian hunter. There were false claims that he had killed dozens of natives. He may have only killed one in self-defense. Said Boone of the Indians, "they have been kinder to me than the whites."

Boone has since been honored on a postage stamp and with a commemorative half dollar. He has had numerous places named after him. He has also been the inspiration or subject of numerous novels and comic strips. A movie was made about him in 1936, and a popular television series in the 1960s, where Fess Parker played him. It must be noted, Daniel Boone was not a big man, as the show's theme song claimed. And he never wore a coonskin cap.

Daniel Boone's original grave in Marthasville, Missouri.

Carter Braxton
(1736 – 1797)

Most Descendants

Buried at Unknown Location,
Chericoke Plantation, King William County, Virginia.

Declaration of Independence • Continental Congress

Carter Braxton was a conservative Virginia plantation owner and merchant, a grandson of Robert "King" Carter, one of the wealthiest landowners in Virginia's history. Braxton was active in Virginia's legislature for a quarter century and during a brief stint in the Continental Congress, signed the Declaration of Independence. He fathered eighteen children via his two wives and is believed to have more descendants than any other Founding Father.

Braxton, born on September 10, 1736, at Newington Plantation in King and Queen County, Virginia, was the youngest of two sons of George Braxton. His mother, the youngest daughter of Robert "King" Carter, died as a consequence of his birth. Both the mother's and father's families were very wealthy landowners on Virginia's Northern Neck and were active in the colony's legislature.

Braxton's father died when he was 13, leaving him and his siblings orphaned. He and his brother George, the heir to the estate, were raised by neighbors and tutored privately. Braxton entered the College of William and Mary in 1755. That year, he married Judith Robinson of

Carter Braxton

Middlesex County, Virginia, the niece of the Speaker of the House of Burgesses, John Robinson. The marriage lasted only two years when she died in childbirth during the birth of their second daughter. For about four years, Braxton, a widower, traveled to England, with daughters Mary and Judith, where he mixed with high society and gained a reputation for extravagance.

Braxton returned to Virginia in 1760 and moved into Elsing Green, an estate in King William County overlooking the Pamunkey River that his brother had built for him while he was overseas. Braxton then married Elizabeth Corbin in 1761, with whom he had sixteen children, ten of whom survived to adulthood. He also entered the House of Burgesses, serving until 1785, except for a brief time as county sheriff.

On October 3, 1761, Braxton's brother George died in his 28th year, leaving him the entire estate. Unfortunately, it was saddled with significant debts, and the family lost Newington. Apparently, some malfeasance kept up the Braxtons' lifestyle, as it was revealed in the 1766 John Robinson estate scandal that they were the largest beneficiaries of the late speaker's interest-free loans of redeemed paper money supposed to have been destroyed. Ultimately, Braxon still owned over 12,000 acres and approximately 165 slaves. Braxton purchased a small schooner and became engaged in trade between the West Indies and the colonies. In 1767, the Braxtons moved to Chericoke, a new home built a few miles northwest of Elsing Green.

Despite his long affinity for England and high culture, Braxton turned against the motherland in 1769 when he sided with his fellow Virginians in signing the Virginia Resolves against parliamentary meddling, and the First Virginia Association, a nonimportation agreement protesting the Townshend duties. However, Braxton did not sign on to the Second and Third Virginia Associations that would have expanded the boycotts. However, in 1774, he joined the Fourth Virginia Association authorizing committees of safety and local militia and joined the Virginia Committee of Safety.

After Patrick Henry's "Give me liberty or give me death!" speech in Richmond on March 23, 1775, Lord Dunmore, the Royal Governor of Virginia, became very concerned about the potential for armed rebellion. The day after Lexington and Concord, on April 21, 1775, though news had not reached Virginia of the shots fired, Lord Dunmore ordered the Royal Marines to remove the gunpowder and flintlocks from the armory in Williamsburg. This caused outrage among the colonists, who threatened a military uprising. Braxton helped negotiate a settlement between fellow member of the House of Burgesses, Patrick Henry, and his father-in-law, Richard Corbin, who was the Deputy Collector of Royal Revenue. This averted the crisis by paying for the powder taken, but it was only a few weeks until Dunmore fled on June 8, and the royal government collapsed.

On October 22, 1775, Peyton Randolph passed away in Philadelphia while serving as president of the Continental Congress. On December 15, 1775, the Virginia legislature selected Braxton to succeed Randolph. He arrived in Philadelphia in February 1776, critical of the independence movement and worried that France would take over the colonies. Braxton served until August and ultimately warmed to the idea, signing the Declaration of Independence that summer.

Braxton returned home and was thanked, along with Thomas Jefferson, by the House of Burgesses for his services. Just before Christmas 1776, Chericoke burned to the ground, and the family moved to Grove House, West Point, Virginia. Braxton continued his representation in the legislature, opposing the Lee family since their involvement in the Robinson estate scandal, and sparring with Arthur Lee in the press. Braxton was most involved with tax moratoriums and debt relief measures.

Regarding the American Revolution, Braxton loaned money and funded shipping and privateering activities. With a consortium of patriotic planters, he traded tobacco and corned meat abroad to secure arms, ammunition, wheat, salt, cloth, and other trade goods. During this time, the British captured his ships and destroyed his plantations. He was censured by Congress in 1780 for his role in the *Phoenix* affair of 1777 when his privateer seized a neutral Portuguese vessel from Brazil, causing a diplomatic incident.

By the end of the war, Braxton had accumulated considerable debt and had to consolidate his holdings, selling most of his land and slaves. In 1787, he settled into a rented rowhouse in Richmond to clear the debt to the Robinson estate. He was also embroiled in a lengthy lawsuit with Robert Morris, who eventually declared bankruptcy. During this difficult time, Braxton served on the Virginia Council of State from 1786 to 1791 and again from 1794 until his death.

Carter Braxton died in Richmond on October 10, 1797. According to family tradition, the sheriff was at the door trying to collect debts when Braxton expired. His body was buried at Chericoke, which had been rebuilt in 1781 and given to a son. Wrote Dr. Benjamin Rush of Braxton:

> He was not deficient in political information but was suspected of being less detached than he should be from British prejudices. He was an agreeable and sensible speaker and in private life, an accomplished gentleman.

Elizabeth Braxton lived until July 5, 1814. Many of the children of Braxton's eighteen offspring fought in the Civil War for the Confederacy, including Majors Carter Moore Braxton, Tomlinson Braxton, and Elliott Muse Braxton. General Braxton Bragg was named for Carter Braxton but was not a relative. Most African Americans with the name Carter Braxton since the end of the Civil War are presumably descendants of slaves from Braxton's plantations.

In 1910, the family graves at Chericoke were exhumed, and the bodies were moved and reinterred at Hollywood Cemetery in Richmond. Unfortunately, Carter Braxton's remains could not be located, so it is assumed he remains at Chericoke, though he is mentioned on the marker in Richmond.

Chericoke remains in private hands. Elsing Green still stands and is open to tourists. Braxton County, West Virginia, was named in his honor, as was the World War II Liberty Ship SS *Carter Braxton*. The Waterman Steamship Company also had a break bulk freighter named the SS *Carter Braxton* in service from the 1960s to the 1980s.

The Newington Archaeological Site was added to the National Register of Historic Places in 2010.

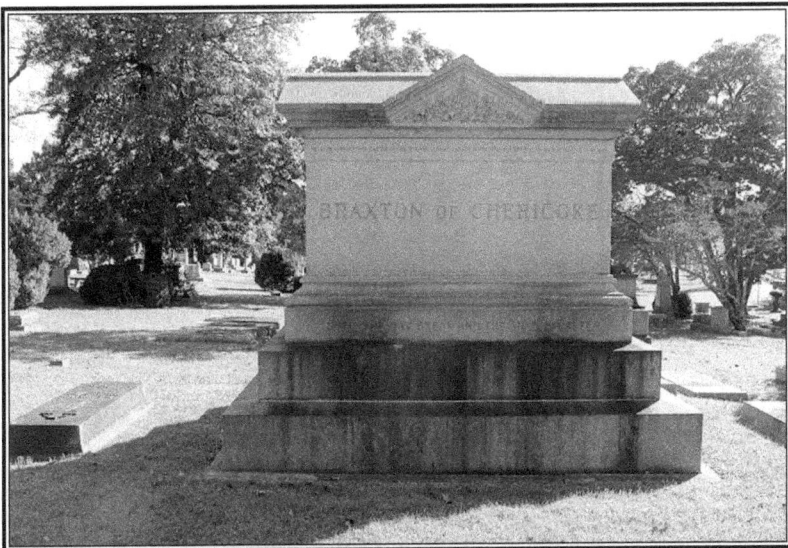

Grave of Carter Braxton

George Rogers Clark
(1752–1818)

Conqueror of the Old Northwest

Buried at Cave Hill Cemetery,
Louisville, Kentucky.

———————

Major General

George Rogers Clark was a Virginia military officer and surveyor who led Patriot forces to victory in what became the Northwest Territory, now most of the Midwestern United States. He led the Virginia militia in Kentucky County (later the state) and won victories at Kaskaskia and Vincennes during the campaign in Illinois. Ultimately, the British ceded the Northwest Territory to the United States at the Treaty of Paris in 1783. Clark was dubbed "Conqueror of the Old Northwest" and "Washington of the West." His younger brother was William Clark of the Lewis and Clark Expedition following the Louisiana Purchase.

———————

Clark was born on November 19, 1752, in Albemarle County, Virginia, near Charlottesville. He was the son of John Clark and his wife, Ann (née Rogers) Clark. Clark was the second of ten children. Five of the six sons were officers during the American Revolution, except for the youngest son, the aforementioned William.

When Clark was very young, in 1756, following the start of the French and Indian War, the family moved east to Caroline County, Virginia, to a 400-acre farm, which later grew to a 2000-acre plantation.

George Rogers Clark

As a lad, his grandfather managed his education. Clark preferred being outdoors and did not take to the classroom. He was tutored at home and attended Donald Robertson's school, where James Madison and John Taylor of Caroline also attended. Clark was then apprenticed to a surveyor and began exploring the land.

At age 19, in 1771, Clark surveyed western Virginia for the first time. The following year, he traveled into the Kentucky region via the Ohio River at Fort Pitt and stayed for two years, surveying the Kanawha River region and learning the natural history and Native tribes of the region.

Meanwhile, following the Treaty of Fort Stanwix in 1768, settlers began entering the area. Unfortunately, not all the tribes with claims to the region were involved in the treaty, and by 1774, hostilities had broken out. Clark was appointed as a captain in the Virginia militia in what became known as Lord Dunmore's War, won by the colonists.

Following the victory, Clark began surveying the Kentucky terri-tory and assisted in organizing Kentucky as a county of Virginia after North Carolinian Richard Henderson purchased the same land from the Cherokee in an illegal treaty. Clark and Gabriel Jones were sent to Williamsburg to petition the Virginia General Assembly to include Kentucky within Virginia. Governor Patrick Henry agreed, and Clark was given five hundred pounds of gunpowder to help defend the settlements. Now 24 at the outset of the American Revolution, Clark outranked older settlers such as Daniel Boone, Benjamin Logan, and James Harrod.

In 1777, without support from the Continental Army, Clark was commissioned as a lieutenant colonel in the Illinois Regiment of the Virginia militia as the leader of a secret expedition to attack British forts north of the Ohio River, specifically the villages of Kaskaskia, Cahokia, and Vincennes. Clark raised troops in Pennsylvania, Virginia, and North Carolina, and headed to Redstone, on the Monongahela River, south of Fort Pitt, in what is now Fayette County, Pennsylvania.

On May 12, 1778, the troop left Redstone and headed down the Monongahela on boats, heading for Fort Henry and Fort Randolph at the mouth of the Kanawha River. They reached the Falls of the Ohio (modern-day Louisville, Kentucky) on June 12 and camped and trained on Corn Island for twelve days.

On June 24, Clark and his brigade floated down the Ohio River to the Mississippi River, where they took Fort Kaskaskia on July 4, 1778, without firing a shot. Captain Joseph Bowman and his men captured Cahokia the next day, also without a shot. Fort Sackville, also known as Vincennes, along the Wabash River, was taken in August, but the British took it back in December. Rather than wait for an attack on Kaskaskia, Clark led a winter march to retake Fort Sackville at Vincennes.

Clark and 170 men left Kaskaskia on February 6, 1779, and trekked overland through melting snow, ice, and freezing rain, arriving at Vincennes on February 23. They laid siege to Fort Sackville and executed five captured Natives with hatchets in view of the fort. Two days later, the British surrendered and Lieutenant Governor Henry Hamilton was captured. News of the victory traveled to General Washington and was mentioned in the discussions with France regarding potential support.

Virginia followed by claiming the Old Northwest region, calling it Illinois County. The victory was the highlight of Clark's career.

In 1780, Clark could not motivate the Kentucky soldiers to head north to attack Fort Detroit, so he continued to defend the Ohio River Valley from the Falls of the Ohio. In June, a mixed British-Indian force attacked from Fort Detroit, capturing two settlements and hundreds of prisoners. In August, Clark led a successful retaliatory strike at the Shawnee village of Peckuwe, near present-day Springfield, Ohio.

During 1781, Governor Thomas Jefferson made Clark a brigadier general responsible for the militia in Kentucky and Illinois counties. Clark prepared to attack Fort Detroit, but the regulars sent by General Washington to assist were defeated in August before they could meet up.

In August 1782, the British and their Native allies again attacked the Kentucky militia, defeating them at the Battle of Blue Licks. Clark was not present and was roundly criticized. Three months later, he led a retaliatory expedition, destroying Native villages along the Great Miami River.

When the Treaty of Paris was signed on September 3, 1783, Britain ceded the Old Northwest Territory to the United States. This doubled the size of the original thirteen colonies, and Clark's victory at Vincennes was romanticized. George Mason dubbed Clark the "Conqueror of the Northwest."

Clark has a reputation as an Indian hater. He proposed raising a force of two thousand soldiers to clean out the Ohio Valley of Natives. He warned them that if they attacked, they "should know that the next thing would be the Tomahawk" with "Your Women & Children given to the Dogs to eat." The expedition was never approved.

Meanwhile, settlers continued to move to the Illinois country and Kentucky. On December 17, 1783, Clark was made the Principal Surveyor of Bounty Lands, and for the next five years, he assisted war veterans with their land grants. However, the relations with the Natives did not improve.

Despite the Treaties of Fort McIntosh (1785) and Fort Finney (1786), which Clark helped negotiate, the Natives continued to attack settlers, killing upwards of 1500 of them. Clark raised an expedition of 1200 drafted men to attack the Natives along the Wabash River, but some of the troops mutinied due to a supply shortage, and Clark turned the brigade around. Afterward, James Wilkinson accused Clark of drunkenness, and Clark's actions were condemned by the Virginia Council. This ended his military career.

In 1787, Clark left Kentucky and moved to Indiana Territory, near present-day Clarksville. He tried to recover expenses owed to him by Virginia, but they refused, claiming his purchases were "fraudulent." Clark struggled with debt. Virginia then followed with "Clark's Grant" of 150,000 acres of land in Indiana, which encompassed what is now Clark County, Indiana, and portions of adjoining counties. However, Clark was unable to develop the land for lack of funds.

In the early twentieth century, Clark's account books were found in Richmond, and they were determined to be complete, sound, and accurate. Thus, he seemed exonerated from "fraudulent" purchases, but this was not official, and a century too late to help Clark.

Desperate to raise some funds, Clark next signed up with the ambassador from France, amid its revolution, to lead an expedition against the Spanish in the southern Mississippi River region. On February 2, 1793, Ambassador Edmond-Charles Genêt appointed Clark "Major General in the Armies of France and Commander-in-chief of the French Revolutionary Legion on the Mississippi River." Clark then began to organize a campaign to take St. Louis, New Madrid, Natchez, and New Orleans. He spent thousands of dollars of his own funds to gather supplies. Clark was also romantically interested in Teresa de Leyba, the sister of Fernando de Leyba, the lieutenant governor of Spanish Louisiana, but this relationship fell apart, and Clark never married everyone.

One year, later, before the expedition could be launched, President Washington forbade it and threatened to send General Anthony Wayne to enforce the ban. The French backed off and canceled the commissions granted to Americans. Clark's efforts to be reimbursed for the supplies went unanswered. Clark's reputation now sunk even lower.

Now in an even deeper hole, Clark's creditors began coming after him with more intensity. Quickly, he transferred ownership of his lands to family and friends to avoid losing them altogether. In the end, after the creditors claimed most of what remained, Clark was left with a small plot at Clarksville.

In 1803, Clark built a small cabin overlooking the Falls of the Ohio. He also purchased a small gristmill nearby operated by two slaves. Over the years, Clark entertained the likes of John Pope, James Audubon, William Clark, Meriweather Lewis, Allan Bowie Magruder, and John P. Campbell. Sadly, his alcoholism continued to plague him as did his anger toward Virginia, the perceived cause of his financial difficulties.

In 1805, Clark was named to the board of directors of the Indiana Canal Company, which planned to build a canal around the Falls of the Ohio. The company collapsed the following year when board members Vice President Aaron Burr and Governor of the Louisianna Territory, James Wilkinson, were arrested for treason. Over $1.2 million in investments went unaccounted for and never found.

Clark stayed here until 1809 when his health began to fail after suffering a severe stroke. Then he fell into a lit fireplace and burned his right leg so severely it had to be amputated. Now immobile, he moved to his sister Lucy Croghan's home at Locust Grove. She was the wife of Major William Croghan.

Finally, in 1812, Virginia granted Clark a pension of $400 per year and granted him a ceremonial sword in recognition of the Revolutionary War services.

On February 13, 1818, Clark suffered another stroke and was buried at Locust Grove Cemetery. In 1869, his remains and those of his family were moved to Cave Hill Cemetery, at Louisville, Kentucky. Said Judge John Rowan at the funeral, "The mighty oak of the forest has fallen ..."

Finally, several years after his death, the government of Virginia began reimbursing Clark's estate, with an initial sum of $30,000. Payments continued to the estate for nearly one hundred years, until 1913.

Clark is remembered in many ways. In 1928, a memorial to him was erected at Vincennes, Indiana. Numerous other statues have been installed throughout the country and Clark's name adorns numerous schools, counties, towns, and streets.

Clark graves

Cyrus Griffin
(1748–1810)

The Last President of Congress

Buried at Bruton Parish Churchyard,
Williamsburg, Virginia.

President of Congress

Cyrus Griffin was an attorney from Farnham, Virginia, who served as a member of the Virginia House of Delegates, the Second Continental Congress, and the Ninth Congress of the Confederation. During the final year of the Continental Congress, Griffin was the last President of Congress, overseeing the transition from the Articles of Confederation to the U.S. Constitution. He was then appointed a federal district judge during the Washington administration and served in that capacity for the rest of his life.

Cyrus Griffin was born on July 16, 1748, in Farnham Parish, along the Rappahannock River, in Virginia, the fourth son of Leroy Griffin, a tobacco farmer, and his wife, Mary Ann (née Bertrand) Griffin, of Huguenot heritage. The Griffin family is believed to be an old Welsh family, possibly descended from the last king of Wales, Llewellyn Griffin, who fell in battle against Edward I of England, in 1282, after a reign of 28 years. The Griffins were early settlers in Virginia, along the tidewater area, in the mid-1600s. Thomas Griffin and his brother Samuel emigrated from Wales and settled along the Rappahannock River. When

Cyrus Griffin

Samuel returned to Wales to inherit their late brother's estate, Thomas remained.

Leroy Griffin died while Cyrus was a child, leaving a portion of his estate to him. These funds were utilized to educate Cyrus in Great Britain. He studied law in Scotland at the University of Edinburgh and met Lady Christina Stuart, the eldest daughter of Charles Stuart, the Sixth Earl of Traquair, circa 1770. When Charles, the patriarch of one of Scotland's noble families, learned of the relationship, he was furious. Griffin was the son of a "lowly" planter from Virginia and an Episcopalian. The Stuarts were devout Roman Catholics. Consumed by passion, the young couple eloped to London, where Griffin continued his legal studies at the Middle Temple.

John Griffin, their first child, was born in 1771 while the couple was still in England. In 1774, Griffin, who had graduated from law school, returned to Virginia to start his practice. He left Christina and young John behind. He returned the following year as the hostilities of the American Revolution commenced. He sought a dowry from his father-in-law but was unsuccessful. While in England, he worked privately to find a way to reconcile the differences between England and her American colonies. He proposed the following ideas in a letter to his friend Lord Dartmouth in London:

- That the Commissioners be instructed to meet either the whole or any number of those men who compose the Congress at any particular place except Philadelphia.
- That when so met and Ceremonies adjusted, they shall begin from the year 1763 and discuss each separate grievance complained of by America.
- That when any point is fully debated the Meeting shall adjourn to the next day; in the meantime, the Commissioners are to determine with themselves how far or whether they shall totally admit the hardship under consideration; such determination to be sent in writing upon the next morning, and by a special Officer, to the aforesaid delegates sitting to receive the same; the delegates to vote by a majority whether the determination of the Commissioners will be satisfactory.
- That if there should be any points upon which The Commissioners and Delegates cannot perfectly agree those points may be referred to the wisdom of the next parliament, and the Colonies to be heard by Counsel in the said parliament.
- That when all matters are finished at this united convention, the Members of the Congress shall return to Philadelphia, and the said Congress shall instantly dissolve themselves.

Frustrated on both fronts, Griffin took his wife and son with him and returned to Virginia in 1775. The Griffins would later have five additional children, totaling four sons and two daughters.

The young attorney soon became involved in state politics. In 1777, he was elected to the Virginia House of Delegates. Then, on May 29, 1778, he was elected to the Continental Congress. He attended sessions from August 19 to October 21 and about December 23 to December 31, 1778. During this time, he observed the machinations and posturing of members of Congress, writing to Thomas Jefferson about his worries and the perceived lack of honor and patriotism.

Griffin was re-elected to the Continental Congress on June 18, 1779, and served through the year's end. He was corresponding with Benjamin Franklin, who was in France, regarding his dowry's settlement. Franklin had taken up representing Griffin to Charles Stuart. Franklin and Stuart were likely acquainted when Franklin visited Scotland in 1771 with Henry Marchant. Thanks to Franklin, Charles Stuart and his daughter reconciled before his death in 1779. In letters to Franklin, Griffin thanked him for his assistance and worried about the Continental Congress's precarious financial position. He also complained that he is often Virginia's lone representative. Griffin held on, serving through June 1780, when he finally resigned. One of his final letters was to Thomas Jefferson regarding the need to increase the military presence in Virginia as it was invaded by the British.

During his final days in Congress, Griffin was appointed a judge of the Court of Appeals in Cases of Capture, which handled cases involving ships and cargo seized during the war. Griffin served on this court longer than anyone else in its short history, remaining until the Continental Congress ended its jurisdiction in 1787. In 1782, he was one of the committee members appointed by Congress to oversee a settlement of the boundary dispute between Pennsylvania and Connecticut regarding the Wyoming Valley.

Griffin's attempts to return to Congress failed in 1783, 1784, and 1786, when he lost elections. He also failed to gain a seat on the Virginia Executive Council in 1786. However, he did win a seat in the Virginia House of Delegates, which he held until January 1787. Then, on October 23, 1787, Griffin was elected to Congress after the U.S. Constitution had been signed while the state ratification process was underway. Sadly, during this time, his son Cyrus Jr. died.

On January 22, 1788, Griffin was elected the fifteenth and final President of Congress, succeeding Arthur St. Clair. He then presided over the Continental Congress's final year as it transitioned to the new constitutional government. His term ended on November 16, 1788.

Griffin lost the election to be a member of the First Congress in the House of Representatives. However, he was elected to the Virginia Executive Council. Before he could take his seat in August 1789, President Washington appointed Griffin to a three-man commission established to negotiate with the Creek Indians. He served on this commission with David Humphreys and Benjamin Lincoln.

Next, Griffin expressed his desire to Washington to become the next U.S. ambassador to France, succeeding Thomas Jefferson. However, Washington had other ideas. During a Senate recess, he appointed Griffin to be a judge on the newly created United States District Court for the District of Virginia. Washington nominated him again on February 8, 1790, and Griffin was approved by the Senate two days later. He served in this capacity for the remainder of his life. In 1807, Griffin may have attended or presided over the treason trial of Vice President Aaron Burr.

The decrepit stone marking Cyrus Griffin in Williamsburg.

He also officiated the libel trial of newspaper editor James T. Callendar, embroiled in controversies against Thomas Jefferson.

Cyrus Griffin died at Yorktown, Virginia, on December 14, 1810, at 62. An article in the Baltimore newspaper *The Federal Republican* stated, "He was a gentleman highly respected for his eminent virtues, his integrity, and independence. He has filled many public appointments, and always with honor to himself, and with advantage to the country."

Griffin was laid to rest next to his wife, who had predeceased him in 1807, in the Bruton Churchyard in Williamsburg, Virginia. Both lie in a nondescript, unmarked tomb.

Benjamin Harrison V
(1726 – 1791)

Father and Great-Grandfather of Presidents

Buried at Berkeley Plantation,
Charles City County, Virginia.

———•◦•———

Continental Association • Declaration of Independence

Benjamin Harrison V was a wealthy planter and merchant who served in the colonial Virginia legislature, followed by the Continental Congress, where he signed the Continental Association, Olive Branch Petition, and the Declaration of Independence. He was then governor of Virginia. Harrison's son, William Henry Harrison, became the 9th President of the United States. His great-grandson and namesake became the 23rd President of the United States.

———◈◦◈———

Benjamin Harrison V was born April 5, 1726, in Charles City County, Virginia, to Benjamin Harrison IV and his wife, Anne (née Carter), the oldest of ten children. The family lived on the Berkeley Plantation, built by the elder Harrison. He was a member of the Virginia House of Burgesses, as had been the prior three generations of Benjamin Harrisons going back to the colonist in 1630, only 25 years after Jamestown. The elder Harrison was also a major in the Charles City County militia and the local sheriff. Benjamin's mother was the daughter of Robert "King" Carter, the president and treasurer of the Virginia colonial council, who served as the acting governor of the colony and the rector of the College of William and Mary.

Benjamin Harrison

On July 12, 1745, the elder Harrison and daughter Hannah were killed at Berkeley Manor by a lightning strike as they shut an upstairs window during a storm. Now the patriarch of the family at only 19, Benjamin inherited Berkeley and several other plantations in the area in addition to thousands of acres, a fishery, and a grist mill. His siblings split six other plantations.

In 1748, Harrison married Elizabeth Bassett, the daughter of Colonel William Bassett and Elizabeth (Churchill) Bassett. Together they had eight children. The eldest daughter, Lucy Bassett Harrison, married Peyton Randolph. Daughter Anne Bassett Harrison married David Coupland. Benjamin Harrison VI was a successful merchant and member of the Virginia House of Delegates. Carter Bassett Harrison served in the Virginia House of Delegates and the US House of Representatives. Their youngest child, William Henry Harrison, became a popular general known as the Hero of Tippecanoe. He was then a congressional delegate for the Northwest Territory, the Governor of the Indiana Territory, and a US senator. In the 1840 United States presidential election, running under the slogan "Tippecanoe and Tyler Too," William Henry Harrison, the first candidate of the Whig party, defeated Martin Van Buren. He fell ill after his inauguration and died just one month into his presidency.

Benjamin Harrison had attended the College of William and Mary at Williamsburg. He did not graduate. Instead, pursuing a life in politics. His brothers also served their communities. Carter Henry Harrison became a leader in Cumberland County, west of Richmond. Nathaniel Harrison was elected to the House of Burgesses and then the Virginia Senate. Henry Harrison fought in the French and Indian War. Charles became a brigadier general during the American Revolution.

In 1749, Harrison was elected to the Virginia House of Burgesses, serving for over a quarter-century representing Surry and Charles City Counties. In 1768, Harrison was appointed to a committee to draft Virginia's response to the Townshend Acts, protesting the tax on tea and other imports as payment for the French and Indian War. In 1770, he was a signer of the association boycotting British imports. He also sponsored a bill declaring Parliament's laws illegal if they were passed without the consent of the colonial legislature. In 1772, Harrison served as a justice and was one of several gentlemen who purchased a building for the city of Williamsburg to use as its courthouse. Also that year, he and Thomas Jefferson were among a group of six Virginia delegates who prepared and delivered an address to King George calling for an end to the importation of sales from Africa. The King rejected this, and both Harrison and Jefferson continued to own slaves.

On March 12, 1773, Richard Henry Lee, the recipient of a report from Samuel Adams in Massachusetts, offered resolutions to establish a Committee of Correspondence to cooperate with that colony and others. Upon the adoption of Lee's resolutions, the Virginia Assembly appointed the following members to act as a Committee of Correspondence: Peyton Randolph, Robert Carter Nicholas, Richard Bland, Richard Henry Lee, Benjamin Harrison, Edmond Pendleton, Patrick Henry, Dudley Digges, Dabney Carr, Archibald Cary, and Thomas Jefferson.

In December 1773, the colonists of Boston protested the tax on British tea by destroying cargos in the harbor. Harrison initially thought the colonists should reimburse the East India Company for the damages caused by the Boston Tea Party, but the subsequent Intolerable Acts hardened his position against the King and Parliament. On May 24, 1774, he and 88 other Virginia delegates signed an association condemning Parliament and invited other colonies to convene a Continental Congress. Harrison was selected to be one of Virginia's delegates to this new body August 5, 1774, to travel to Philadelphia. Said Edmund Randolph of him, "A favorite of the day was Benjamin Harrison. With strong sense and a temper not disposed to compromise with ministerial power, he scruples not to utter any untruth. During a long service in the House of Burgesses, his frankness, though sometimes tinctured with bitterness, has been the source of considerable attachment."

Harrison arrived in Philadelphia on September 2, 1774, for the First Continental Congress. John Adams, in his diary of the first days of the Congress, wrote that day of his first meeting with the Virginian:

> 2 [Sept]. Friday. Dined at Mr. Thomas Mifflin's, with Mr. Lynch, Mr. Middleton, and the two Rutledges [Edward and John, both of South Carolina] with their ladies. The two Rutledges are good lawyers. Governor [Stephen] Hopkins and Governor [Samuel] Ward [both of Rhode Island] were in company. Mr. [Thomas] Lynch [of South Carolina] gave us a sentiment: "The brave Dantzickers, who declare they will be free in the face of the greatest monarch in Europe." We were very sociable and happy. After coffee, we went to the tavern, where we were introduced to Peyton Randolph, Esquire, Speaker of Virginia, Colonel Harrison, Richard Henry Lee, Esquire, and Colonel Bland. Randolph is a large, well-looking man; Lee is a tall, spare man; Bland is a learned, bookish man. These gentlemen from Virginia appear to be the most spirited and consistent of any. Harrison said he would have come on foot rather than not come. Bland said he would have gone, upon this occasion, if it had been to Jericho.

Benjamin Harrison V (1726–1791)

On September 6, 1774, recording his observations of some of the early debates in Congress regarding proportional representation, delegate James Duane of New York wrote:

> Col. Harrison from Virginia insisted strongly on the injustice that Virginia should have no greater Weight in the determination than one of the smallest Colonies. That he should be censured by his constituents and unable to excuse his want of attention to their Interest. And that he was very apprehensive that if such a disrespect should be put upon his Country—men we shoud [*sic*] never see them at another Convention.

Around that time, Silas Deane of Connecticut wrote to his wife about the delegates:

> I gave you the character of the South Carolina delegates, or rather a sketch. I will now pursue the plan I designed. Mr. Randolph, our worthy President, may be rising of sixty, of noble appearance, and presides with dignity. Col. Harrison may be fifty; an uncommonly large man and appears rather rough in his address and speech.

Harrison aligned with John Hancock, while Richard Henry Lee aligned with John Adams. Adams later described Harrison in his diary variously as "another Sir John Falstaff," "obscene," "profane," and "impious." The next month, Harrison was one of the delegates to sign the Continental Association, implementing a trade boycott with Britain.

The following May, when Harrison arrived for the Second Continental Congress, he roomed with his brother-in-law, Peyton Randolph, and George Washington, until he left to take command of the Continental Army in June. On July 5, 1775, Harrison was one of the signers of the Olive Branch Petition, albeit reluctant. The two had a war of words during the debate. Dickinson remarked he disapproved of only one word in the petition, "congress." Replied Harrison, "There is but one word in the paper, Mr. President, of which I do approve, and that is the word 'congress.'" The King rebuffed the chance of reconciliation.

That October, Peyton Randolph died suddenly from a heart attack while dining with Thomas Jefferson. This left Harrison alone in his Philadelphia residence. Harrison now kept busy with military affairs, corresponding with his former roommate. In November, he traveled with Washington, Benjamin Franklin, and Thomas Lynch to Cambridge to inspect the army's condition. Congress now realized the need to increase the number of troops and to increase their pay.

Nearing July 1776, Harrison was chairman of the Committee of the Whole, presiding over the final debates of the Lee Resolution, expressing a desire for independence. Harrison oversaw the amendments of the Declaration of Independence after the Committee of Five presented the draft of the Declaration of Independence. Harrison reported the approved final form of the document on July 4, giving its final reading. Congress then unanimously adopted it. Harrison was one of the signers the next month. At that event, many of the signers were nervous. Benjamin Rush described a "pensive and awful silence" as the delegates believed they were signing their death warrants. He then described how Harrison, known for his sense of humor, lightened the mood. Rush wrote that the corpulent Harrison approached the slender Elbridge Gerry when he was about to sign and said, "I shall have a great advantage over you, Mr. Gerry, when we are all hung for what we are now doing. From the size and weight of my body, I shall die in a few minutes and be with the angels, but from the lightness of your body, you will dance in the air an hour or two before you are dead."

During 1777, Harrison was named to the Committee of Secret Correspondence for the Congress, whose objective was to communicate securely with colonial agents in Britain. He was also named the Chairman of the Board of War, overseeing the army's movements and the exchange of prisoners. During this time, he had a spat with Washington over the commission of the Marquis de Lafayette. Harrison insisted the position was only honorary and without pay. He also endorsed a controversial idea that the Quakers had the right not to bear arms based on their religious beliefs.

In September 1777, Congress fled Philadelphia, stopping briefly in Lancaster before heading to York, Pennsylvania. There, they debated the

Articles of Confederation. Again, Harrison argued for greater representation for the larger states, like Virginia. Concerned about his properties back home and not making headway with the Articles, Harrison headed back to Virginia in October. There, he returned to the Virginia House and was elected Speaker. There, he focused on providing for the defense and western land interests.

In January 1781, Benedict Arnold, now on the British side, led an invasion of the James River in Virginia. Harrison arranged for his family to flee Berkeley before Arnold arrived and destroyed most of Harrison's possessions and a large portion of his house. Arnold also burned all the family portraits so that no likeness of the family would survive. Fortunately, the Harrisons escaped with their lives. Soon after the British left, the Harrisons returned and began rebuilding. Harrison returned to his duties, helping supply the army.

Following the victory at Yorktown in October 1781, Harrison was elected the fifth Governor of Virginia. During this time, he focused on the financial difficulties the state was facing at that time. This included negotiating with the native tribes rather than warring with them. This did not please George Rogers Clark, who wanted to secure more western territory. Harrison served as governor through 1784, after which he returned to the House of Delegates.

Elizabeth Harrison, Harrison's wife of over forty years, died in September 1787. In June 1788, Harrison was named to the state constitutional convention to ratify the new US Constitution. Harrison spoke against it because it did not clarify the rights for which they had fought. He voted against its ratification, but when it was known that reforms would be included after all the states passed it, Harrison became a supporter.

Harrison, suffering from chronic gout and other ailments, continued in his service in the Virginia House until his death at Berkeley on April 24, 1791, while celebrating his re-election. Harrison was laid to rest in the family burial ground at Berkeley.

As mentioned previously, Harrison's youngest son, William Henry Harrison, became the 9th President of the United States in 1841. He served only one month before he died. In 1846, Harrison's heirs asked the US government to reimburse the family for pay, bounty land, and other expenses incurred by Harrison from the American Revolution to his death. Harrison's great-grandson, Benjamin Harrison, served in the US Senate from Indiana (1881–87) and as the 23rd President of the United States (1889–93). His great-great-grandson, William Henry Harrison (1896–1990), served in the US House of Representatives (1951–55, 1961–65) as a Republican from Wyoming. A residence hall at the College of William and Mary is named for Harrison. Also, a bridge spanning the James River near Hopewell, Virginia, bears his name.

In the foreword of the book *The Harrisons* by Ross F. Lockridge, the author writes, "The Harrison family is justly believed to have given more distinguished men to American history than any other family."

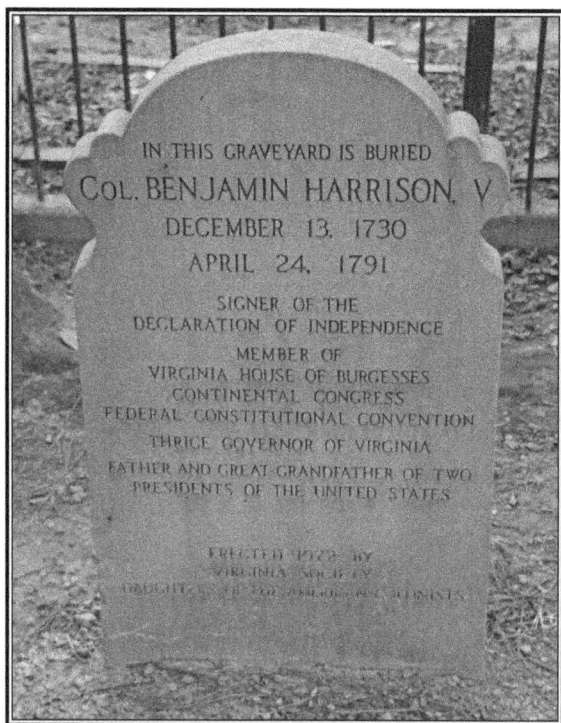

The grave of Benjamin Harrison.

John Harvie
(1742–1807)

Friend of Jefferson

Buried at Hollywood Cemetery,
Richmond, Virginia.

Articles of Confederation

John Harvie was an attorney and builder from Virginia, the son of Thomas Jefferson's guardian, John Harvie Sr. He served in the Virginia House of Delegates and operated a prison camp during the Revolution. He was elected to the Second Continental Congress, where he signed the Articles of Confederation. Later, he was the mayor of Richmond and was a lifelong friend of Jefferson.

Harvie, born in 1742 at the family's 2500-acre estate, Belmont Plantation, in Albemarle County, Virginia, was the son of Scottish immigrant John Harvie Sr., a planter, and his wife, Martha (née Gaines) Harvie. When Thomas Jefferson's father, Peter Jefferson, died in 1757 during Thomas's fourteenth year, neighbor John Harvie Sr. became his legal guardian. Young Harvie and Jefferson, only a year apart, became like brothers and were close for the rest of their lives.

Harvie studied law and was admitted to the Virginia bar. In 1767, he inherited Belmont Plantation when his father died and continued to live there. His mother moved to Georgia with his eight siblings, leaving the 25-year-old to run the estate. Harvie then married Margaret Morton

JOHN HARVIE.
Signer of the Articles of Confederation.

John Harvie

Jones, the daughter of Gabriel Jones, a longtime member of the House of Burgesses, and Margaret Strother Morton Jones. The couple had seven children: Lewis, John, Edwin, Jacquelin, Gabriella, Emily, and Julia.

Prior to the American Revolution, Harvie grew his business interests. He was also one of the first lawyers to practice at the Albermarle bar. In 1774, following what was later called Dunmore's War, he helped negotiate a peace treaty with the Shawnee following the Battle of Point Pleasant, which occurred in what is now West Virginia.

When Governor Dunmore abolished the House of Burgesses, Harvie was elected to Virginia's new assembly, the Virginia House of Delegates. He attended in 1775 and 1776 and was elected to the Second Continental Congress on behalf of Virginia. He was also a colonel in the Virginia militia in 1776 and helped to organize and purchase supplies.

While in the Continental Congress at York, Pennsylvania, Harvie worked on the Articles of Confederation. He also served on the Board of War for the Congress and inspected the camp at Valley Forge in the Winter of 1777/78. Congress was very concerned about the conditions there. Harvie said to Washington, "My dear General, if you had given some explanation, all these rumors [denigrating Washington] would have been silenced a long time ago."

Harvie signed the Articles on July 9, 1778, and promptly resigned from the Congress afterward. He also procured from Richard Anderson a 240-acre property west of Charlottesville called The Barracks. There, he established a prison camp that held 6000 Hessians and British soldiers by January 1779. The camp had brick buildings to house the troops as well as animals, poultry, gardens, and other outbuildings. Some of the prisoners deserted and headed into the hills. There, they married Native American women. When the camp closed in November 1780, the remaining soldiers were moved north.

In 1780, Harvie was appointed the registrar of Virginia's Land Office and moved to Richmond. He oversaw transactions in the Northwest Territory, western Virginia, Ohio, and Kentucky.

Harvie was elected the mayor of Richmond, Virginia, from 1785 to 1786. His holdings included the magnificent Belmont plantation, as well as the estates at Pen Park and The Barracks. In 1789, he was a presidential elector.

In 1798, Harvie added Judge Bushrod Washington's Belvidere estate in Richmond. Some compared it to Mount Vernon and said it was "an extremely handsome house, and of decidedly superior architecture, being beautifully proportioned."

Harvie died from injuries sustained following the fall from the roof of a building he was inspecting that was under construction. He passed on February 6, 1807, and was buried at Belvidere, which later became part of Hollywood Cemetery in Richmond.

Harvie is remembered by a street in Richmond. Jacquelin Street was named after his son, General Jacquelin Harvie. In 1982, Harvie descendant James Beverly Harvie Jr. placed a plaque near his ancestor's grave, which reads: "Within, and without, these walls rest members of the family of Col. John Harvie, 1742–1807. A guardian of Thomas Jefferson, and signers of the Articles of Confederation and the Bill of Rights. Here, too, lie his son, Jacquelin, and Mary, his wife, daughter of Chief Justice John Marshall. This area, part of the Harvie lands, became Hollywood Cemetery in 1847."

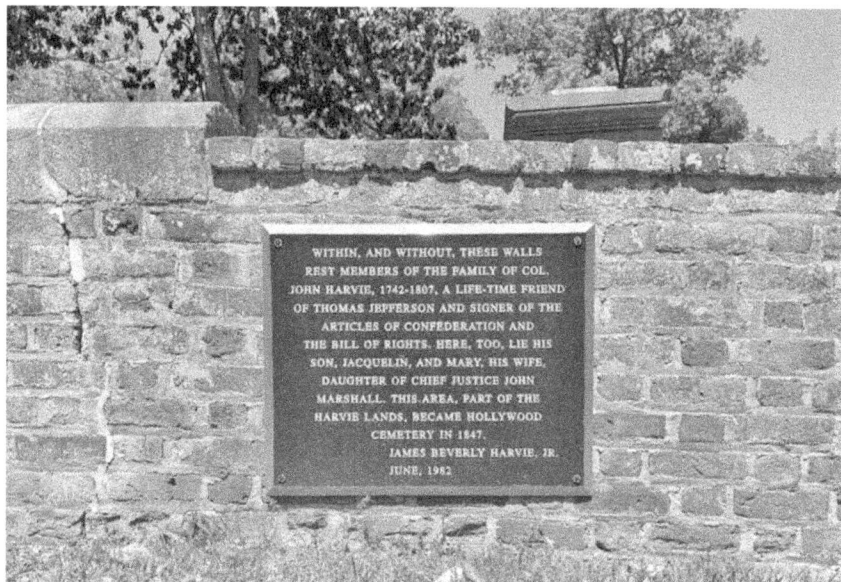

WITHIN, AND WITHOUT, THESE WALLS REST MEMBERS OF THE FAMILY OF COL. JOHN HARVIE, 1742-1807, A LIFE-TIME FRIEND OF THOMAS JEFFERSON AND SIGNER OF THE ARTICLES OF CONFEDERATION AND THE BILL OF RIGHTS. HERE, TOO, LIE HIS SON, JACQUELIN, AND MARY, HIS WIFE, DAUGHTER OF CHIEF JUSTICE JOHN MARSHALL. THIS AREA, PART OF THE HARVIE LANDS, BECAME HOLLYWOOD CEMETERY IN 1847.
JAMES BEVERLY HARVIE, JR.
JUNE, 1982

The Harvie family crypt is within these walls.

Patrick Henry
(1736 – 1799)

Revolutionary Orator

Buried at Henry Cemetery,
Aspen, Virginia .

———•◆•———

Continental Congress • Continental Association

This founder joined the American Revolutionary cause early. He served in the Virginia House of Burgesses, where he became known for his inflammatory orations against the Stamp Act of 1765. He represented Virginia in the First Continental Congress, where he helped draft the Petition to the King. As a member of the body, he signed the Continental Association. After the Revolution, he served as the first and post-colonial Governor of Virginia. He feared a strong federal government, and he declined an appointment to serve as a delegate to the 1787 Constitutional Convention. He was a fierce opponent of the ratification of the Constitution that convention produced. American school children have long learned of him through a speech he delivered on March 23, 1775, to the Virginia House of Delegates, where he said, "Is life so dear or peace so sweet, as to be purchased at the price of chains and slavery? Forbid it, Almighty God! I know not what course others may take, but as for me, give me liberty or give me death." His name was Patrick Henry.

———◆———

Henry was born in Hanover County, Virginia, on May 29, 1736. His father was John Henry, who was born in Scotland but made his way to

Patrick Henry

Virginia when he was in his mid-twenties. He found work as a surveyor's assistant while acquiring land of his own. After twenty years, he owned more than 23,000 acres. His mother was Sarah Winston Syme, who was a widow from a prominent family. Henry attended a local school for a few years, but his formal education came mostly from his father. Jon Kukla, in this biography, *Patrick Henry Champion of Liberty*, notes that Henry's boyhood friends remember that he was "remarkably fond of hunting, fishing, and playing on the violin."

During Henry's childhood years a religious movement known as the Great Awakening occurred. Religion played a key role in his life as both his father and the uncle he was named after were devout Anglicans. His exposure to ministers preaching helped shape what would become the technique he would use as an adult in delivering speeches. He concluded that oratory should aim at the heart and not rely solely on reason.

At the age of fifteen, Henry went to work as a clerk in a local store. Having gained this experience, he and his brother William went into business by themselves, opening their own store. In a short time, the business failed.

In 1754, Henry married Sarah Shelton. As a wedding gift, the bride's father gave the couple a 300-acre farm and six slaves. Henry attempted to work the land with the slaves, but this was a period of drought in Virginia. Then the main house burned down, and Henry had had enough. He moved to the Hanover Tavern, which his father-in-law owned. Henry worked at the tavern, acting as a host and entertaining guests playing the fiddle.

In 1760, Henry decided to study law. He was self-taught and he convinced a panel of Virginia attorneys that he was capable and was admitted to the bar. He opened a law practice that proved successful as he worked in the courts of Hanover and surrounding counties.

The case that cemented Henry's reputation as an attorney was the Parson's Cause. Droughts in Virginia had led to increased prices for tobacco. The Virginia House of Burgesses passed the Two Penny Act, which allowed tobacco debts to be paid at the rate of two pence per pound. The payees included the Anglican clergy. Several ministers appealed to the Board of Trade in London. The Board overruled the Virginia House. The clergymen filed suits for back pay, but only one of them, the Reverend James Maury, was successful, and a jury was appointed to assess and fix damages. After evidence was presented proving the facts at issue, Henry took the floor and gave a one-hour speech. He argued that the veto of the Two Penny Act by the English government and the King, who Henry called a "tyrant," had forfeited his right to his subjects' obedience. He also criticized the clergy for challenging a law aimed at bringing economic relief to the community. The opposing counsel then accused Henry of treason, but he continued his presentation, urging the jury to assess damages at one farthing. The jury deliberated for a short time before fixing the damages at one penny. The local community viewed Henry as a hero, and after the conclusion of the case, Henry became even busier, adding 164 clients for which he would provide legal representation. More importantly, as pointed out by Henry's biographer, Jon Kukla, Henry would transfer the lessons of the Parsons Cause in his arguments against the British government's passage of the Stamp Act.

VIRGINIA PATRIOTS

On March 22, 1765, the British Parliament passed the Stamp Act. The act imposed a tax on all paper documents in the colonies and was the first internal tax levied by the British government on the American colonists. Henry was sworn-in to the Virginian legislature on May 20, 1765. Colonial resistance to Parliament's action was growing and Henry wasted no time in becoming one of the leaders opposing the Stamp Act. On May 29, he introduced the Virginia Stamp Act Resolves. The resolution maintained that the colonists enjoyed the same rights as the populous of the mother country. That taxes can only be enacted by the people's elected representatives. Finally, it stated that only the Virginia General Assembly had the right to tax.

The Resolves were printed in various newspapers around the colonies. In addition, Governor Francis Fauquier sent a report to the Board of Trade. He reported that "Very indecent language was used by Mr. Henry." The governor was successful in keeping the resolutions out of the *Virginia Gazette*. By August, the Resolves reached London. The *London Gazette* reported that "Mr. Henry has lately blazed out in the Assembly where he compared George III to a Tarquin, a Caesar, a Charles the First, threatening him with a Brutus, or an Oliver Cromwell." The Resolves established Henry as one of the first revolutionaries in the colonies.

Opposition to the Stamp Act grew steadily, and by early 1766, many of the stamp distributors had resigned their commissions as crowds of people threatened harm to them personally and to their property. Colonial resistance made it impossible for the British to enforce the act, and later, in 1766, Parliament repealed it. At the same time, they passed the Declaratory Act, which maintained that Parliament had the authority to pass laws governing the colonies.

In the years following the repeal of the Stamp Act, tensions between the English government and the American colonies continued to rise. In 1770, after the Boston Massacre, Henry and other Virginians established an intercolonial Committee of Correspondence. Parliament's passage of the Coercive Acts following the Boston Tea Party and the subsequent closing of the Boston Harbor resulted in uniting the colonies in their resistance.

The First Continental Congress convened on September 5, 1774, in Philadelphia. Henry attended as one of Virginia's representatives. Henry's oratorical skills were impressive, but as Kukla points out in his biography, "the delegates placed greater weight on his ideas. He served on several important committees, and on the second day of the Congress he showed his ability as a speaker when he argued that old governments and colonial boundaries were no more. "The distinctions between Virginians, Pennsylvanians, New Yorkers, and New Englanders are no more. I am not a Virginian but an American." The meeting's main accomplishment was the adoption of the Continental Association, patterned after the Virginia Association. This pact established the nonimportation of British goods that would begin on December 1, 1774, unless Parliament rescinded the Intolerable Acts. It was also decided that a second Congress would meet the following year if the American grievances were not addressed. News of the Association reached King George III, who declared the colonies were "in a state of rebellion." Similarly, Lord Dartmouth, the secretary of state for American affairs, stated, "Everyone who signed it was guilty of treason." Having been accused of treason for more than a decade, Henry was probably unfazed. When Congress adjourned, Henry returned to Virginia. He never again served in a continental or national office.

In January 1775, Peyton Randolph called the Second Virginia Convention whose main purpose was to select delegates to the Second Continental Congress scheduled to be held in May. The convention lasted from March 20 to the 27th. On the convention's fourth day, Henry put forth three resolutions. The resolutions called for the establishment of a well-regulated militia. The third resolution stated, "Resolved therefore that this colony be immediately put into a posture of defense, that a committee be appointed to prepare a plan for embodying, arming, and disciplining such a number of men as may be sufficient for that purpose." This resolution sparked a spirited debate.

The opposition to the proposal argued that it was a "prophesy of war," and it would be seen as Virginia appearing to invite armed conflict. As told by Kukla, when Henry took the floor to respond those in attendance described him starting calmly praising the patriotism of the opposition while noting that his opinions were "the very opposite to theirs." Henry asked how best Americans could resist British oppression. He ridiculed those who favored petitioning the King, saying previous petitions had been disregarded: "And we have been spurned with contempt from the foot of the throne." When he paused, some members murmured, "Peace! Peace! Henry answered, "Gentlemen May cry Peace, Peace, but there is no peace." He noted that "Our brethren are already in the field." He slipped into the posture of a helpless slave so effectively that onlookers perceived manacles "almost visible" on his wrists. Henry asked, "Is life so dear or peace so sweet as to be purchased at the price of chains and slavery?" Raising his eyes and hands toward heaven, he continued, "Forbid it, Almighty God! I know not what course others may take, but as for me . . . give me liberty, or give me death!" The resolutions passed by a close vote of 65 to 60.

In May of 1776, Henry was once again a delegate this time to the Fifth Virginia Convention. Here, he introduced a motion declaring Virginia independent and urging the Continental Congress to declare all the colonies free of the rule of England. When he took the floor to speak, Edmund Randolph said he "appeared in an element for which he was born." The motion passed unanimously. The convention then passed a constitution creating Virginia's government and Henry was elected as the first post-independence Governor.

It was ironic that Henry was elected governor since he had opposed the limited power given to the executive office under the new Virginia constitution. Indeed, he was little more than a figurehead as the real power to govern resided in the House of Delegates. He corresponded regularly with Washington relative to the Revolutionary War effort. He worked at recruiting troops for Washington, but again, these efforts were hampered by, among other factors, the weakness of his office. In December of 1776, the news that the British had occupied Philadelphia reached Virginia, and the General Assembly responded by granting Henry temporary emergency powers. This may have resulted in a rift with Thomas Jefferson, which never healed as he felt Henry was trying to set himself up as a dictator.

Henry would serve until 1779. In 1778, he sent an appeal to Congress saying that naval aid was needed to protect Chesapeake Bay.

Congress did not act, and in May of 1779, British ships entered the bay and captured Suffolk and Portsmouth, where troops destroyed valuable supplies. Soon after, Henry left office. Thomas Jefferson succeeded him.

By this time, Henry had been married twice. First to Sarah Shelton in 1754. The couple had six children before she passed away in 1775. In 1777, he married Dorothea Dandridge. This coupling would produce eleven children, two of whom died very young. After serving as governor, Henry and his family moved to Leatherwood Plantation in Henry County which had recently been created and named for him.

At Leatherwood, Henry served on the county court. He turned down the opportunity to be elected to Congress. He did serve for a short time in the Virginia House of Delegates where he opposed a plan to impose certain taxes. Health problems forced him to leave Richmond and return home. In 1781, as the Revolutionary War moved south and the British occupied Richmond, Henry was active in recruiting soldiers to defend the state. By this time, the state government had moved to Charlottesville and was nearly captured when the British invaded that city; however, the lawmakers were successful in escaping to Staunton. Jefferson fled to a farm he owned in Bedford County, which resulted in Henry and other legislators calling for an inquiry into his conduct. This further deepened the animosity between Jefferson and Henry.

With the American victory at Yorktown, the Revolutionary War ended. Henry continued to represent his county as a delegate through 1784, when, once again, he was elected governor, serving from 1784 through 1786. The Virginian legislature passed a law to acquire new arms for the militia and Henry was active in attempting to acquire these arms from France. He also sought to improve Virginia's development, supporting the construction of canals. His efforts met with mixed results. It was Patrick Henry, acting in his capacity as governor, who signed Virginia's circular letter in February 1786 inviting the other twelve states to send delegates to attend the Annapolis Convention. The main accomplishment of this gathering was to call for a subsequent convention to meet in Philadelphia in 1787 the nation's Constitutional Convention.

Upon his return to Mount Vernon, after presiding over the Constitutional Convention, George Washington wasted no time in sending Henry a copy of the proposed Constitution. As explained by Kukla in his Henry biography, the document was accompanied by a letter in which Washington acknowledged that the proposal wasn't perfect but that he believed "it is the best that could be obtained at this time." Washington was probably disappointed by Henry's reply when he stated, "I have to lament that I cannot bring my Mind to accord with the proposed Constitution," adding, "The Concern I feel on this Account is really greater than I am able to express."

It is somewhat ironic that the man who years earlier declared himself to be an American and not a Virginian now opposed a measure designed to make the nation more than a confederation of states. Over time Henry had lost faith and trust in the northern states. Among other things, he blamed Congress for not supplying the troops necessary to protect Virginians who were settling in the Ohio River Valley. At the Virginia Ratifying Convention, he took the position that the Constitution gave the power to govern to too few, and he noted that it lacked a Bill of Rights and failed to protect individual liberty. On June 25, 1788, Virginia voted in favor of ratification.

Henry returned to the House of Delegates where he was successful in defeating James Madison, a strong supporter of the Constitution, in his effort to become a Senator from Virginia. He also served as one of Virginia's presidential electors, casting his vote for George Washington and John Adams.

Henry removed himself from the political stage until 1799, when Washington convinced him to return after the controversial Kentucky and Virginia Resolutions had passed. These acts were a response to the Alien and Sedition Acts of 1798, and they favored state action against the unconstitutional acts of the federal government and took the position that secession might be necessary. At this point, Henry argued that if a people are oppressed, they should overthrow the government, but he cautioned that it should not occur if there are other means to address the issue and find a remedy. He also warned that "you can never exchange the present government but for a monarchy." Henry once again won the election to the House of Delegates but passed away at his plantation on June 6, 1799, before the assembly convened. He was 63 years of age.

Henry sealed a small envelope before his passing, inside of which was a message saying that whether America's independence would be a blessing, or a curse would depend on the use of the people of the blessings God has bestowed on us. He urged proactive virtue in thyself and encourage it in others. He was laid to rest at Henry Cemetery in Aspen, Virginia.

Grave of Patrick Henry

James Armistead Lafayette
(1748 or 1760 – circa 1830)

Lafayette's Double Agent

Buried at Unknown Location
New Kent County, Virginia

———•◦•———

Spy

James, later known as James Armistead Lafayette or just James Lafayette, was a slave of African descent in Kent County, Virginia, who served in the Continental Army under the Marquis de Lafayette in the latter years of the American Revolution. Gaining the trust of Benedict Arnold and Lord Charles Cornwallis, James was a double agent, feeding false information to the British and intelligence reports to the Americans leading up to the decisive Battle of Yorktown.

———•◦•———

James was born in either 1748 or 1760 in Kent County, Virginia, on the plantation owned by Colonel John Armistead. Unlike most slaves, James was taught to read and write. Sometime before Colonel Armistead's death in 1779, James was given to the colonel's son, William Armistead, the local commissary of military supplies, to be his personal manservant. James was the first slave owned by William.

During the American Revolution, between 5,000 and 8,000 free and enslaved Black men fought for the Patriots, amounting to about three percent of the estimated 230,000 soldiers who served. Early in the war, General Washington, a slaveowner, was uncomfortable with

James Armistead Lafayette (1748 or 1760 – circa 1830)

James Armistead Lafayette

permitting armed Blacks in the armed forces. On July 10, 1775, he barred any additional Blacks from joining them. However, by 1778, at the urgings of others, Washington gradually changed his position. The Marquise de Lafayette, an ardent abolitionist, was one officer who supported permitting enslaved and freed Africans to take up arms and did so openly in his corps.

Upon hearing of Lafayette's openness to Blacks, James requested and was granted permission by his master, a supporter of the Patriot cause, to serve in the Continental Army. In 1781, still enslaved, James joined Lafayette's division and was initially ordered to carry information between the French units. Soon, though, Lafayette realized James's potential to be a spy. Lafayette suggested that James pose as a runaway and seek to infiltrate the British Army.

In November 1775, Lord Dunmore, the colonial Governor of Virginia, issued a proclamation that any slave who fought in the British Army would be emancipated. In the subsequent years, it is estimated that over 100,000 slaves escaped bondage by fleeing to British lines. With this apparent desire and his knowledge of the local roads and terrain in Virginia, Lord Cornwallis was quick to trust James, permitting him in the headquarters. Cornwallis assigned James to spy for Brigadier General Benedict Arnold, himself a recent turncoat. Arnold asked James to spy on the Americans, especially the Marquise de Lafayette! Thus, James shuttled back and forth between the camps, providing Arnold and Cornwallis with false information about the Americans while sharing true information about his adversaries with Lafayette.

In the summer of 1781, General Washington asked Lafayette for any intelligence he had on the positions, equipment, and potential strategies of the British troops. Lafayette sent James to gather this information. James reported back on July 31, 1781, about Cornwallis's movement of 10,000 troops from Portsmouth, Virginia, to Yorktown, Virginia. Washington and French General Rochambeau were then able to devise a blockade and bombardment of Cornwallis, leading to his defeat on October 19, 1781. When Lord Cornwallis surrendered at Lafayette's headquarters, he was stunned to see James, whom he considered his trusted personal slave, among the Americans.

After the war, despite Virginia's manumission act in 1782 granting freedom to slaves who fought in the Revolution, James remained the property of William Armistead. He was restricted by a 1783 law regarding only freeing enslaved service members who had been issued firearms and had served as substitutes for their masters. Because James had been a spy and not a soldier, he did not carry a gun, and was thus not eligible.

Unfairly overlooked, James petitioned the Virginia Assembly for his freedom. In 1784, the Marquise de Lafayette wrote a letter on his behalf detailing James's service to the cause, saying that James had rendered "services to me while I had the honor to command in this state. His intelligence from the enemy's camp were industriously collected and more faithfully delivered. He properly acquitted himself with some important commissions I gave him and appears to me entitled to every reward his situation can admit of." However, despite his master, William Armistead, a member of the House of Delegates, promoting the measure, it took until January 9, 1787, for the governor and both houses to grant his manumission. For the rest of his life, James appended Lafayette to his name in honor of his friend who had vouched for him. Note that others later appended Armistead to him, a name he never used in his lifetime.

James Lafayette, now a freeman, purchased a forty-acre farm in New Kent County, Virginia, in 1816. He was twice married, raised a family, and became relatively wealthy. He also owned slaves. In 1819, after years of petitioning for it, James began receiving a pension as a Revolutionary War veteran from Virginia.

While touring all twenty-four of the United States in 1824 on the invitation of President James Monroe, Lafayette visited Virginia, stopping at Yorktown, Washington's tomb at Mount Vernon, and gave a speech to the General Assembly at the capital of Richmond. While in Richmond, Lafayette saw James in the crowd and ordered his carriage to stop. He exited the coach and called out to James. The two warmly embraced in front of an astonished crowd. It was unusual behavior in Antebellum Virginia.

James returned to his farm afterward. He lived until either 1830 or 1832, dying in Baltimore, Maryland, or New Kent County, Virginia. His burial location is lost.

James Lafayette is honored in several, mostly nondescript, ways. A Black servant depicted in a portrait of Lafayette by Jean-Baptiste Le Paon in 1785 might be James. He was mentioned in James E. Heath's two-volume historical novel *Edge Hill: or the Family of the Fitz Royals*, published in 1828. A portrait of him was painted by John Blennerhassett Martin at the time of the book. The Lafayette memorial at Prospect Park in Brooklyn, New York, might include a figure of James. A Virginia historical marker was erected in 1997 at the New Kent County courthouse honoring him.

Francis Lightfoot Lee
(1734–1797)

Virginia Congressman

Buried at Tayloe Family Burial Ground,
Warsaw, Virginia.

———•◦•———

Declaration of Independence • Articles of Confederation

Francis Lightfoot Lee, the brother of Richard Henry Lee and cousin of "Light Horse Harry" Lee, was a Continental Congressman who signed the Declaration of Independence and Articles of Confederation. He was also a member of the Virginia state House of Delegates and the state Senate.

———◈◦◈———

Lee was born October 14, 1734, at "Machadoc," later known as "Burnt House Field," in Hague, Westmoreland County, Virginia. After the completion of "Stratford Hall," in Westmoreland County, Virginia, a few years later, the family moved there. He was the fourth son, and one of eleven children, of Thomas Lee, a planter in Virginia, and his wife Hannah Harrison (née Ludwell) Lee. Thomas Lee was a leading Virginia planter with over 30,000 acres of land prior to his death in 1750.

Francis was taught by private tutors at "Stratford Hall." When his parents died in 1750, the estate was left to the older children, leaving out Francis and his younger siblings. His oldest brother, Phillip Lee, controlled his parents' assets. Francis and the younger children sued in court for a portion but lost. Eventually, Francis reconciled with his brother and was granted one of the family estates in Loudon County.

Portrait of Francis Lightfoot Lee, artist unknown.

Lee then got into politics and ran for a seat in the Virginia House of Burgesses in which he served from 1758 to 1768. Lee's first patriotic action was his protest of the Stamp Act. He signed the Westmoreland Resolves which was a business protest of the act that played a part in the repeal of the Stamp Act.

In 1769, Lee married his second cousin Rebecca Plater Tayloe and moved from Loudon to Richmond County where his father-in-law had gifted them "Menokin" plantation on which to reside. He was again elected to the House of Burgesses but only served occasionally. From 1770 to 1774, he was a justice of the peace for his new Richmond County. He also served in that position for Loudon County in 1771.

In March 1775, a convention of delegates gathered in Richmond to organize for the Revolution. Lee was one of the delegates from Richmond. In August of that year, Lee was appointed to the Continental Congress and moved to Philadelphia with his wife, staying with his sister and brother-in-law, William Shippen, who himself was later a Continental Congressman. Lee served in the Continental Congress into 1779, but biographers recorded that he rarely spoke, though his opinions were valued.

The Reverend Charles Goodrich wrote in 1842,

During his attendance upon this body, he seldom took part in the public discussions, but few surpassed him in his warmth of patriotism, and in his zeal to urge forward those measures which contributed to the success of the American arms, and the independence of the country. To his brother, Richard Henry Lee, the high honor was allotted of bringing forward the momentous question of independence, and to him, and his associates in that distinguished assembly, the not inferior honor was granted of aiding and supporting and finishing this important work.

Robert T. Conrad added in 1846, "Although not gifted with the powers of oratory, his good sense, extensive reading, and sound and discriminating judgment, made him a useful member of the house."

It is believed Francis Lee signed the Declaration of Independence with many others in August 1776. In an 1821 letter to painter John Trumbull in a Washington newspaper, the artist was critiqued for not including Francis Lee in the painting of the signers, though many who were not present on July 4 were included in it.

Lee continued in the Congress until he resigned in April of 1779, having also signed the Articles of Confederation before

"Mount Airy" Plantation where Francis Lightfoot Lee is buried
(photo by Lawrence Knorr).

they were ratified. He returned to Virginia and served in the state senate for a period, but then retired. In 1788, he clashed with his brother, Richard Henry Lee, when he supported ratification of the Constitution.

Francis Lee died of pleurisy at "Menokin" on January 11, 1797, at the age of 62, only four days after his wife passed. *The American Minerva* newspaper of New York City printed an obituary,

> Died. At his seat in Richmond County, on Wednesday, the 18th ultimo, in the sixty-third year of his age, Francis Lightfoot Lee, Esquire. He was an early, zealous and active friend to the revolution, which established the independence of the United States of America. He was a firm, calm, and enlightened patriot, and a most unequaled social companion.

Lee and his wife were laid to rest at the Tayloe's "Mount Airy" plantation near Warsaw, Virginia. The authors were unable to visit the graves which are on private property posted with a sign threatening gunshots if dust was seen in the driveway.

The grave of Francis Lightfoot Lee.

In 1877, Mark Twain wrote about Lee,

> This man's life-work was so inconspicuous, that his name would now be wholly forgotten, but for one thing—he signed the Declaration of Independence. Yet his life was a most useful and worthy one. It was a good and profitable voyage, though it left no phosphorescent splendors in its wake.

Francis and Rebecca Lee had no children; his namesake Francis Lightfoot Lee II was the son of his brother Richard Henry Lee, and further men of the same name descend from him.

Henry Lee III
(1756–1818)

Lighthorse Harry

Buried at Lee Chapel at Washington and Lee University,
Lexington, Virginia.

----•◦•----

Military

Henry Lee III, known as "Light-Horse Harry" Lee, was a cavalry officer during the American Revolution. He served in the Continental Congress (1785–1788) where he pushed for the reform of the Articles of Confederation. He then served as governor of Virginia and in the U.S. House of Representatives where he is remembered for his eulogy of the late George Washington. He was the father of Robert E. Lee, the Confederate commander in the Civil War.

----▷◦◁----

Henry Lee III was born on January 29, 1756, at "Leesylvania," the family estate near Dumfries, Prince William County, Virginia. He was the son of Henry Giles Lee II and Lucy (née Grymes) Lee. His brother, Charles Lee (1758–1815) served as Attorney General under President George Washington (1795–1797). These Lees were cousins to the Lees of "Stratford Hall" which included Richard Henry Lee and Francis Lightfoot Lee.

Young Henry was tutored at home and then entered the College of New Jersey (now Princeton), graduating in 1773 at the age of 17. He was prepared to go to England to study law, but the onset of the American

Portrait of Henry "Lighthorse Harry" Lee, III, by
William Edward West.

Revolution prevented it. Instead, he received military training and was commissioned as a captain in the Virginia Dragoons on June 18, 1776.

An excellent horseman, Lee was quickly promoted and soon found himself in charge of three troops of cavalry and three companies of infantry dubbed Lee's Legion. At Paulus Hook, near New York harbor, he surprised the enemy post and captured 160 men, bayonets, and ammunition earning the nickname "Light-Horse Harry" and resulting in the gift of a gold medal from Congress—the only such medal given to someone of lower rank than general. This meteoric rise as a young officer led to him being arrogant and intolerant of criticism. He was twice before boards of court-martial.

Now a lieutenant colonel, in 1780 Lee was assigned to the Southern Department under Nathanael Greene. Lee's Legion raided the British outpost of Georgetown, South Carolina with General Francis Marion in January 1781. He acted as the rear guard of the American army, harassing the British as Greene's troops continued a strategic retreat through the Carolinas to cross the Dan River into Virginia in February. He then combined with Francis Marion and Andrew Pickens to capture numerous British outposts in South Carolina and Georgia. Along the way, they terrorized Loyalists throughout the region highlighted by Pyle's Massacre on February 24, 1781. At Guilford Courthouse (March 15, 1781), Lee's troops fought to a draw, but Lee failed to communicate with Greene, leading to a collapse of the lines and an American retreat. Lee then saw action at Eutaw Springs in September 1781. Lee stayed in the service of Greene during the remainder of the successful Southern Campaign and was present at Yorktown for Cornwallis's surrender there.

With the British defeated, Lee resigned his commission and returned to Virginia. There he married his cousin, Matilda Ludwell Lee, known as "Divine Matilda," in 1782. The couple had three children who lived past infancy: Philip Ludwell Lee (1784–1794), Lucy Grymes Lee (1786–1860), and Henry Lee IV (1787–1837). The latter was a historian and author who served as a speechwriter for both John C. Calhoun and presidential candidate Andrew Jackson. He helped to write Jackson's inaugural address.

Now a private citizen, and close friend of George Washington, Lee entered politics and was elected to the Virginia House of Delegates in 1785. On November 15, that body selected him to a seat in the Continental Congress. He attended sessions through 1788, writing that the government was in shambles without proper financing or foreign policy. Wrote historian Thomas Templin in his biography of Lee:

> Lee was, of course, well aware of the condition of the national government before he went to New York to sit in Congress. Even so, he seems to have been shaken by the impotency which he found there. His arrival came at a somewhat inauspicious time: Congress was virtually crippled by the non-attendance of sufficient members to conduct business, and it was engaged in a frustrating discussion of how to deal with the unwillingness of Georgia and New York to consent to a revised impost measure. On 16 February [1785] Lee wrote Washington and Madison on "the dreadful situation of

Lee Chapel at Washington and Lee University in Lexington, Virginia
(photo by Lawrence Knorr).

our federal government," referring to the inertia of Congress, the dreary outlook for obtaining money needed to meet obligations, and the poor diplomatic position of the United States with respect to Britain, the Barbary States, and the western Indians. Lee's appraisal of the government was "its death cannot be very far distant unless immediate and adequate exertions are made by the several states."

Lee pushed for the reform of the Articles of Confederation, which was replaced by the U.S. Constitution. Lee was a delegate to the Virginia convention that ratified the Constitution in 1788.

Lee was greatly affected by the death of his wife in 1790. He grieved and focused on family for nearly two years. Then, he was elected Governor of Virginia in 1792, serving for three years. In 1793, he married Anne Hill Carter with whom they had six children: Algernon Sidney Lee (1795–1796), Charles Carter Lee (1798–1871), Anne Kinloch Lee (1800–1864), Sydney Smith Lee (1802–1869), Robert Edward Lee (1807–1870), and Mildred Lee (1811–1856).

In 1794, President Washington asked Lee to command the nearly 13,000 federal troops to put down the Whiskey Rebellion in western

Pennsylvania. Washington had ridden at the head of the column through Pennsylvania along with Lee. He then handed the army to Alexander Hamilton after they joined up at Fort Cumberland. This rebellion was put down without a loss of life.

In 1798, Lee was appointed Major General, in anticipation of war of France. Later that year, he was elected to the Sixth Congress (1799–1801), where he was best known for the eulogy of the late President Washington, calling him "first in war, first in peace, and first in the hearts of his countrymen."

After leaving Congress, Lee retired to the family estate, "Stratford Hall," in Virginia, but struggled financially due to the Panic of 1796–97 and the bankruptcy of Robert Morris. In 1808, in anticipation of war with Britain, Lee was again commissioned a major general by Thomas Jefferson and he began organizing the Virginia militia. The following year, Lee became bankrupt and served one year in debtors' prison in Montross, Virginia, after which he moved the family to Alexandria, Virginia.

As the War of 1812 was about to break out, Lee appealed to President Madison to serve again in the military, but Madison refused. Around this time, he published his *Memoirs of the War in the Southern Department of the United States* where he recounted his military experiences during the Revolutionary War. During the civil unrest in Baltimore, Maryland in July of 1812, Lee was severely beaten and left for dead on the street. As a Federalist, he and others had opposed the War of 1812 and were present to defend newspaperman and friend Alexander Handon. The group was jailed by Baltimore city officials. A mob led by George Woolslager then broke into the jail, removed the Federalists, and beat and tortured them. One, James Lingan, died.

Lee was greatly affected by his injuries to his body, head, and face, and suffered a speech impediment. He went to the West Indies in 1817, and while returning the following year, stopped to convalesce at his old commander Nathanael Greene's daughter's home near St. Mary's, Georgia. He died there on March 25, 1818, at the age of 62. His body was initially buried in a crypt near the home in Dungeness, Georgia, with full military honors.

In 1862, as Robert E. Lee was reviewing military defenses near Cumberland Island, Georgia, he visited the grave of his father, a man he barely knew. In May 1913, Lee's remains were exhumed and buried next to Robert E. Lee's under the Lee Chapel at Washington and Lee University in Lexington, Virginia.

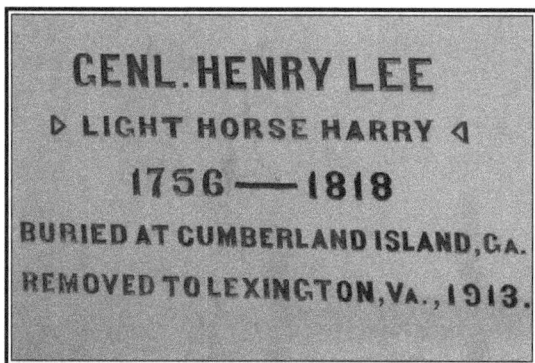

GENL. HENRY LEE
▷ LIGHT HORSE HARRY ◁
1756 —— 1818
BURIED AT CUMBERLAND ISLAND, GA.
REMOVED TO LEXINGTON, VA., 1913.

Crypt of Henry Lee, III, beneath the Lee Chapel, next to his son Robert E. Lee (photo by Lawrence Knorr).

Richard Henry Lee
(1732 – 1794)

Resolution for Independence

Buried at Lee Family Plot,
"Burnt House Field" plantation, Coles Point, Virginia.

———•◦•———

Continental Association • Declaration of Independence
Articles of Confederation • President of Congress

Richard Henry Lee, the brother of Francis Lightfoot Lee and cousin of "Light Horse Harry" Lee, was a Continental Congressman who signed the Continental Association, Declaration of Independence, and Articles of Confederation. He was also the President of Congress (1784–1785). He is best known for proposing the Lee Resolution, the motion in the Continental Congress calling for independence from Great Britain. He was also a United States Senator from (1789–1792).

———•◦•———

Lee was born January 26, 1732, at "Machadoc," later known as "Burnt House Field," in Hague, Westmoreland County, Virginia. He was the fifth son, and one of eleven children, of Thomas Lee, a planter in Virginia, and his wife Hannah Harrison (née Ludwell) Lee. Thomas Lee, the president of the Virginia Colonial Council, was a leading Virginia planter with over 30,000 acres of land prior to his death in 1750. After the completion of "Stratford Hall," in Westmoreland County, Virginia, a few years later, the family moved there.

Richard was taught by private tutors at "Stratford Hall." He was then sent to England to study at Wakefield Academy in Yorkshire. When his

Portrait of Richard Henry Lee by
Charles Willson Peale.

parents died in 1750, his oldest brother, Phillip Lee, urged him to return home, but he refused, instead going on a tour of mainland Europe.

Richard returned to the colonies in 1753 and continued his studies. In 1755, during the French and Indian War, he was named the head of a volunteer militia serving under General Edward Braddock. Fortunately for Lee, Braddock did not utilize his unit and he saw no action nor did he play a role in the fateful Braddock Expedition. Lee married Anne Aylett in December 1757, and settled at his plantation, "Chantilly-on-the Potomac," near "Stratford Hall." Richard and Anne had four children— two sons and two daughters. The following year, while hunting, Lee's gun exploded in his hands, taking all but one finger on his left hand. For the remainder of his life, Lee wore a glove to cover up the wound. Later that same year, Anne Lee died of pleurisy.

In 1764, Lee was named to a committee by the House of Burgesses to send a message to the king calling for an end to harmful economic measures being enacted against the colonies. In February 1766, Lee was one of the leading figures behind the establishment of the Westmoreland Association. One surviving draft of that document in Lee's hand stated,

> . . . the Birthright privilege of every British subject (and of the people of Virginia as being such) founded on Reason, Law, and Compact; that he cannot be legally tried but by his peers; and that he cannot be taxed, but by the consent of a Parliament, in which he is represented by persons chosen by the people. The Stamp Act does absolutely direct the property of the people to be taken from them without their consent.

In 1767, Lee was a justice of the peace in Westmoreland County. The following year, he was elected to the Virginia House of Burgesses, taking the seat of his brother Philip. He served until 1775 along with his brothers Thomas Ludwell Lee and Francis Lightfoot Lee. In this body, he

"Burnt House Field," Lee Family Estate, in Coles Point, Virginia (photo by Lawrence Knorr).

railed against slavery wanting to tax it into oblivion. He believed slaves were entitled to equal freedom and liberty. Such views put him at odds with most of the men in that body. In 1769, Lee married Anne Gaskins Packard, a widow, and together the couple would have three daughters and two sons.

In 1773, Richard Lee was a member of the Virginia Committee of Correspondence along with Peyton Randolph, Robert Carter Nicholas, Richard Bland, Benjamin Harrison, Edmund Pendleton, Patrick Henry, Dudley Digges, Dabney Carr, Archibald Cary, and Thomas Jefferson. The following year, Lee was elected to the Continental Congress where he served until May 1779. During this time, Lee was a signer of the Continental Association, the Declaration of Independence, and the Articles of Confederation.

Regarding independence, Lee was an early and ardent proponent. Following Lexington and Concord, he was still in the minority, but as time went by, more and more delegates joined him. On June 7, 1776, Lee put forth a motion for independence,

> Resolved: That these United Colonies are, and of right ought to be, free and independent States, that they are absolved from all allegiance to the British Crown, and that all political connection between them and the State of Great Britain is, and ought to be, totally dissolved.

There was rancorous opposition to the motion, so much so that the President of Congress, John Hancock, had to table it to avoid a fight. Meanwhile, the Committee of Five including Thomas Jefferson, Ben Franklin, John Adams, Roger Sherman, and Robert Livingston set about drafting a formal declaration. Though absent on July 4th, Richard and his brother Francis returned in August to sign the document, being the only brothers to do so.

Soon after, Lee was accused by John Hancock and Robert Morris of conspiring with John and Samuel Adams to remove Washington as commander of the Continental Army. At this time his brother Arthur Lee was serving as a diplomat to France along with Benjamin Franklin and

Silas Deane. Arthur informed Richard that Deane was using the position for his own personal gain. Richard took to the floor of the Congress and denounced Deane and moved to recall him from Paris. Deane did so and defended himself before Congress, causing a rift in the body. This forced Henry Laurens to resign as the President of Congress. In retaliation, Deane accused the entire Lee family of corruption. Lee's friend, John Adams, wrote to Samuel Cooper in February 1779 a defense of the Lee family,

> The complaint against the family of Lees is a very extraordinary thing indeed. I am no idolater of that family or any other, but I believe their greatest fault is having more men of merit in it than any other family; and if that family fails the American cause, or grows unpopular among their fellow-citizens, I know not what family or what person will stand the test.

Lee soon resigned from his seat in the Congress and returned to Virginia where he continued to serve in the state House of Delegates and as a colonel in the Westmoreland militia.

In 1784, Colonel Arthur Campbell wrote to encourage Lee to reconsider service in the Continental Congress. He did so and was elected in June 1784. At that point, Thomas Mifflin resigned as President of Congress and the position was vacant for several months. In November, Lee agreed to take the position and held it until November 1785 when he was succeeded by John Hancock. During his tenure, the U.S. dollar was established as the currency of the land, tied to the Spanish dollar (piece of eight). The Congress also unsuccessfully worked to sell western lands to cover the war debts.

Lee was a delegate to the Virginia convention to ratify the U.S. Constitution in 1788 and was one of two senators appointed to serve in the first Congress. He did so from March 1789 until he resigned in October 1792 as his health was beginning to fail.

Richard Henry Lee died on June 19, 1794, at the age of 62. Lee was buried at the Lee family estate's graveyard at "Burnt House Field," in Coles Point, Virginia. His gravestone reads,

Here was buried Richard Henry Lee, of Virginia, 1732–1794. Author of the Westmoreland Resolutions of 1766. Mover of the Resolution for Independence. Signer of the Declaration of Independence. President of the Continental Congress. United States Senator from Virginia.

Many public schools across the nation are named after Lee. In 1941, a liberty ship bore his name.

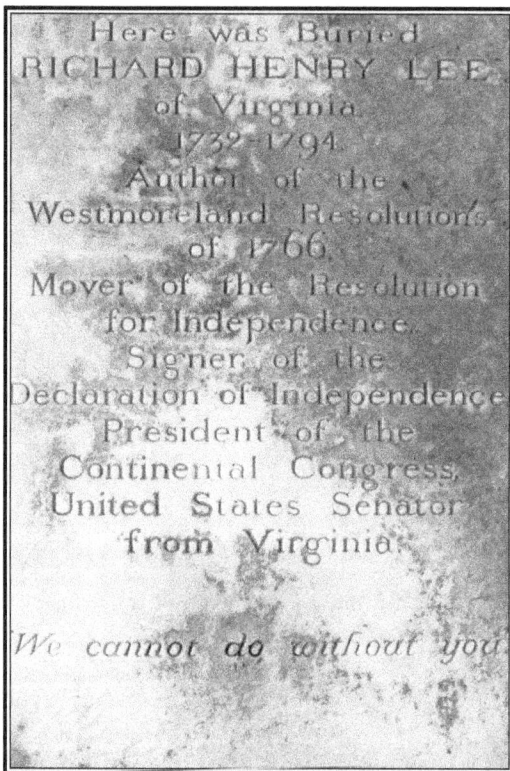

Detail from Richard Henry Lee's gravestone
(photo by Lawrence Knorr).

John Marshall
(1755 – 1835)

The Great Chief Justice

Buried at Shockoe Hill Cemetery,
Richmond, Virginia.

Supreme Court — Secretary of State — House of Representatives

John Marshall was a Virginia attorney who was a distant relation of Thomas Jefferson. Marshall is one of few Americans who has served in all three branches of the Federal Government. He served briefly as Secretary of State under John Adams and was a US House Representative from Virginia, prior to becoming the longest-tenured and most influential Chief Justice of the Supreme Court in American history.

Marshall was born in a two-room log cabin on September 24, 1755, in Germantown, Fauquier County, Virginia, near present-day Midland, the son of Thomas Marshall, a surveyor and land agent for Lord Fairfax, and Mary Randolph (née Kieth) Marshall, who was the daughter of Thomas Randolph of Tuckahoe Plantation and a second cousin of Thomas Jefferson. In the 1760s, the increasing family moved to Markham, Virginia. John Marshall was the first of fifteen children. Younger brother James Markham Marshall later became a federal judge. Marshall was also the first cousin of Kentucky Senator Humphrey Marshall, and first cousin, three generations removed, of George C. Marshall, Army Chief of Staff, Secretary of Defense, and Secretary of State.

Marshall was not formally educated, except for one year during which he befriended James Monroe. Otherwise, Marshall was encouraged to

John Marshall

read widely and greatly respected his parents. Father Thomas Marshall purchased the Oak Hill Plantation in the early 1770s, and the family moved there.

At the outbreak of the American Revolution in 1775, Thomas and John enrolled in the 3rd Virginia Regiment. The following year, Marshall was a lieutenant in the Continental Army's 11th Virginia Regiment. He fought at the Battles of Brandywine, Germantown, and Monmouth, and was at Valley Forge during the bitter winter of 1777/8.

Following his furlough from the Army, Marshall attended the College of William and Mary and read law under George Wythe. He was admitted to the bar in 1780 and after a brief return to the Army in the Yorktown area, he was elected to the Virginia House of Delegates in 1782. During his time in Yorktown, he met Mary Ambler, the daughter of Jaquelyn "Jack" Ambler, a member if Virginia's Council of State. He married Mary on January 3, 1783.

At the Virginia House, Marshall was well-connected thanks to friends such as James Monroe and Richard Henry Lee and his father-in-law. Soon, Marshall, too, was elected to the Council of State as his father-in-law became Treasurer. Marshall was the youngest to serve on the Council up to that point, at only 28.

In 1785, Marshall also became the Recorded of the Richmond City Hustings Court and began to build his law practice. In 1786, he purchased his cousin's, Edmund Randolph's, practice when he became Governor of Virginia. His reputation grew, especially when he represented the heirs of Lord Fairfax in *Hite v. Fairfax*.

A strong supporter of the new Constitution, Marshall was elected to the Virginia Ratifying Convention in 1788, siding with James Madison on convincing delegates to approve, winning 89 to 79.

During the early days of the Washington Administration, Marshall rebuffed an offer to become the US Attorney for Virginia despite being confirmed by the Senate. Instead, he focused on his law practice and building the Federalist Party within the state, counter to his cousin, Thomas Jefferson, who led the opposing Democratic-Republicans. He was also the Grand Master of Masons in Virginia during 1794 and 1795. He again rebuffed Washington in 1795 when asked to be US Attorney General. Instead, he continued to serve Virginia in a variety of roles. The following year, he appeared before the same court to argue the *Ware v. Hylton* case, and though he lost, he acquitted himself well.

Early in the Adams administration, in 1797, the relations with Revolutionary France were tenuous and Marshall was one of three delegates, including Charles Cotesworth Pinckney and Elbridge Gerry, who were sent to France to negotiate. After a fifteen-minute meeting with French Foreign Minister Talleyrand, they were met by three of Talleyrand's subordinates who demanded bribes. Pinckney and Gerry left immediately, but Marshall lingered for two months and sent secret correspondence to Adams. He then returned to the US in April 1798, and Congress demanded to see the correspondence. When the public learned of the bribes in what was known as the XYZ Affair, Congress imposed an embargo on France in July 1798 and the two sides harassed each other's ships. During this Quasi-War, Marshall supported most of Congress's measures but opposed the Alien and Sedition Acts that were meant to suppress dissent.

In September 1798, at the urging of George Washington and Patrick Henry and owing to his popularity in the XYZ Affair, Marshall ran for and won Virginia's 13th Congressional District, defeating Democratic-Republican incumbent John Clopton. During the campaign, Marshall declined an appointment to be an associate justice on the US Supreme Court. Instead, his friend, Bushrod Washington, the nephew of the president, was selected.

Next, in May 1800, President Adams first nominated Marshall to be the Secretary of War but changed his mind and switched to Secretary of State. He was confirmed by the Senate on May 13, 1800, and took office on June 6, replacing the fired Timothy Pickering. Adams now wanted peace with France. This was achieved in October.

The 1800 presidential election was a very close affair, with the Democratic-Republican ticket of Thomas Jefferson and Aaron Burr defeating the incumbent Federalist ticket of John Adams and Charles Cotesworth Pinckney, 73 electoral votes to 65. In the Electoral College of the time, the top two vote-getters would be president and vice-president, respectively. During the 1796 election, Adams and Jefferson, despite being in separate parties, were elected. This time, each elector had two votes and placed one vote each on their two candidates on the ticket. The plan was to have one or two electors not vote for the intended vice presidential candidate, instead voting for a candidate unlikely to win. But this did not happen as expected, and both Jefferson and Burr had the same number of electoral votes. The election then went to the House of Representatives where each state had one vote. After thirty-six ballots and a deal struck by Alexander Hamilton, Jefferson was named the President and Burr the Vice President.

Meanwhile, during this lame-duck period, President Adams and the Congress passed the Judiciary Act of 1801, later known as the Midnight Judges Act, expanding the federal judiciary and reducing the number of Supreme Court justices from six to five upon the next vacancy. This was intended to deny the next president an opportunity to appoint a justice until a second vacancy had occurred. However, Chief Justice Oliver Ellsworth suddenly resigned due to poor health, Adams needed to replace him. At first, he offered it to John Jay, who had held the position in the past. Jay refused. Secretary of State Marshall suggested that Justice William Paterson be elevated to Chief Justice, but Adams rejected the idea, stating, "I believe I must nominate you."

The Senate confirmed Marshall on January 27, 1801, and he took office on February 4. President Adams also requested he stay on as Secretary of State until the inauguration on March 4. Of course, it had yet to be determined who would be President. The 36th ballot occurred two weeks later, on February 17. Thus, had that ballot not been successful, and the controversy continued, it was possible that Marshall, still next in line at Secretary of State and now Chief Justice, would have been the active president. Marshall now set about implementing the Midnight Judges Act and its appointments. Critics saw this as a court-packing maneuver as judges had to be approved for the new lower-level courts. Marshall raced against the inauguration clock and ran out of time on the last day to complete them all due to not being able to "carry all the documents."

Marshall quickly rose to prominence in his new role. He changed the way rulings were presented, preferring to provide a majority opinion rather than seriatim opinions (from each justice). He implemented the process of judicial review via the 1803 case of *Marbury v. Madison*, creating the independent judiciary. The Supreme Court helped define the separation of powers, permitting the court to strike down federal and state laws deemed unconstitutional.

Prior to Marshall, the Supreme Court had made only 63 decisions. For the next thirty-four years, Marshall oversaw over 1000 decisions, laying the precedents for countless future cases. It was the practice of the time that the justices worked in their circuits for six months out of the year and sequestered in Washington, DC, the rest of the time, staying in the same hotel. There, they would meet together acting as their own clerks and hammer out their decisions. Marshall was known for building consensus and allowing his justices to form their majority opinion before weighing in. Justice Oliver Wolcott described Marshall's knack for "putting his own ideas into the minds of others, unconsciously to them."

One of the Associate Justices of the Supreme Court was Marshall's friend, Bushrod Washington, the nephew of the former president. The nephew inherited the papers of his uncle and asked Marshall to assist in writing a biography of George Washington based on them. The first two volumes were completed in 1804, with the set growing to five volumes when complete.

During his tenure on the court, Marshall also oversaw the impeachment hearing of Associate Justice Samuel Chase, who was acquitted by the Senate, the treason trial of Aaron Burr, for allegedly attempting to create an independent republic in the western United States. When Thomas Jefferson declared his correspondence with General James Wilkinson as protected by executive privilege, Marshall ruled most of the evidence against Burr was inadmissible, and Burr was acquitted, much to the chagrin of Jefferson and the Democratic-Republicans. Towards the end of his tenure, during the Jackson administration, Marshall was often at odds with the President, a Democrat, and found his influence waning as his colleagues on the court were gradually replaced. After the passing of Associate Justice Bushrod Washington, Marshall was alone of all the justices he had originally worked with.

In December 1831, Marshall's wife, Polly passed away at Richmond, Virginia. Marshall focused on an abridgment of his Washington biography for schools, completing it in 1833. However, his health was gradually failing, and on July 6, 1835, he died in Philadelphia while seeking medical treatment. He was 79 years old and had served as the Chief Justice for 34 years. Oddly, Marshall's son Thomas had died in Baltimore two days earlier when a chimney collapsed in a storm while he was on his way to Philadelphia to be with his father. Marshall never learned of this death.

The Liberty Bell was rung at Philadelphia in honor of his death. One story claimed it was the last time the bell was rung because it cracked. Marshall was returned to Richmond where he was interred at Shockoe Hill Cemetery, next to his wife.

Marshall was the last surviving cabinet member from the first Adams administration and the last to have served in the 1700s. Andrew Jackson nominated Roger Taney to replace him.

Marshall is remembered in many ways. His homestead and birthplace are national historic parks. He has appeared on currency, postage stamps, painting, and statues, and his name has been used for many places and institutions. If it has Marshall in the name, it is likely named for John Marshall.

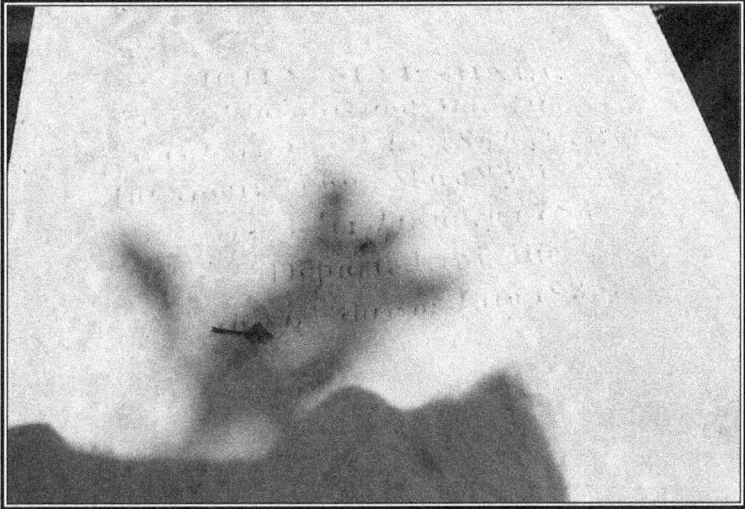

Grave of John Marshall

George Mason
(1725–1792)

"The Father of the Bill of Rights"

Buried at Mason Family Cemetery
Lorton, Virginia

——————

U.S. Constitution • U.S. Bill of Rights

A recent biographer described this man as America's most unappreci-
ated and underestimated Founding Father. His writings influenced
both American political thinking and events including the American
Revolution itself. He was the principal author of the Virginia Declaration
of Rights upon which the United States Bill of Rights was based. He was
a delegate to the 1787 Constitutional Convention in Philadelphia and
one of the three men who refused to sign the finished product put forth
by that gathering. His opposition to the Constitution cost him his long
friendship with his Virginia neighbor, George Washington. His name
was George Mason.

——————

Mason was born on December 11, 1725, at his father's Dogue's
Head plantation in Stafford County, Virginia. Both his father (George
Mason III) and his mother, Ann, came from well-off families whose
forefathers had been among Virginia's oldest settlers. In 1735, Mason's
father drowned at the age of forty-nine when his boat capsized as he was
crossing the Potomac River. His mother proved to be a major force in his
coming of age. She would wake him at dawn and send him to begin his
chores on the plantation. Since he was the first-born son, it was assumed

George Mason

that Mason would eventually run the plantation operations. With his father's death, he assumed burdens that normally he would not have had to shoulder at such a youthful age. It is not an exaggeration to say he became an adult sooner than most his age at the time.

According to his biographer, William G. Hyland Jr., in *George Mason: The Founding Father Who Gave Us the Bill of Rights,* Mason developed a toughness because of the responsibilities he had to assume. He also turned to older men to act as his mentors. One of these was his uncle, John Mercer. It was Mercer who took on the responsibility for Mason's formal education. The foundations for Mason's career in politics were instilled by Mercer. Mercer was a lawyer who owned a private library that contained at least fifteen hundred volumes. These works contained books by Pope, Milton, Swift, and Voltaire. Reading these authors and others resulted in Mason developing a passion for individual freedom. In addition, the influence of Mercer's library would be seen in Mason's contributions to the Constitution and the Declaration of Independence.

When Mason reached the age of twenty-one, he inherited his father's lands which included a large estate as well as thousands of acres of farmland located in Maryland and Virginia. His inheritance also included lands yet to be cleared in the western part of the country and his father's slaves, which numbered approximately three hundred. Material things were not all he inherited; as his biographer notes, "Mason inherited one quality from both of his parents that became his most important character trait: perseverance. Mason was also taught by his mother and father and later by his tutors and mentors that a Virginia gentleman owed service to his family, to his country, and to his colony—in that order."

After taking possession of his inheritance, Mason returned to his childhood home at Dogue's Neck, where he built Gunston Hall, the home he would live in for the next forty years. In 1750 he married Ann Eilbeck, described as beautiful and charming. Her earlier suitors included George Washington, though all he found was disappointment. The Mason marriage would last twenty-three years and produce nine children that would live to adulthood. At the end of her final pregnancy, she gave birth to twin boys prematurely. Both died the day after they entered this world. She never recovered her health, and she passed away three months later. Mason's grief over her death was evidenced by the fact that he stayed in his room or his study for the next week. Though he would remarry in 1780, he would wear black mourning clothes for the rest of his life.

Even prior to his marriage, Mason had begun his public career. He was one of the largest local landowners, and that came with duties and obligations. In 1747, he was named to the Fairfax County Court. He also served as a vestryman from 1749 to 1785. In addition, he was a colonel in the local militia and in 1758, he was elected to the House of Burgesses.

Even though he had a large family to raise, a plantation to run and his public service, Mason suffered from ill health for much of his adult life. He himself attributed his many ailments to the "gout," which at the time was a catch-all phrase. In Mason's case, his gout affected his feet, hands, and stomach. At times he was only able to walk with the aid of crutches. His ailments also made it difficult for him to travel. As a result, he spent many hours in his study pouring over political philosophy. The conclusions he drew from these studies would make themselves evident in his later writings.

Despite his ailments, Mason found that he had to continue in the public arena to aid in the protest of British taxes. He edited the Nonimportation Association Agreement for Virginia in 1769. Next, he wrote the twenty-four articles protesting the English government that became the Fairfax Resolves. Here he took on the British Parliament's authority over the colony of Virginia. He was also elected to represent Fairfax County in the House of Burgesses. It was as a member of this body that Mason was the main author of both the Virginia Declaration of Rights and the Constitution of Virginia. In1776. Thomas Jefferson would paraphrase some of Mason's work in the Declaration of Independence. Mason wrote, "That all men are created equally born free and independent and have certain inherent natural rights among which are the enjoyment of life and liberty with the means of acquiring and possessing property and pursuing and obtaining happiness and safety." His Declaration of Rights was approved on June 12, 1776, and appeared in the *Virginia Gazette* and the *Philadelphia Gazette*. This was a full month prior to Jefferson's draft of the Declaration of Independence. According to his biographer "the case can be made that George Mason should be credited with an original draft of what ultimately became the famed Declaration of Independence."

In his Mason biography, William G. Hyland Jr. notes that John Locke's *Second Treatise on Civil Government*, written in 1690, was a major influence on Mason's own works. Locke took the position that the purpose of government was to protect the natural rights, liberty, and property of the people. That a contract existed between the government and the people, and if that contract was broken, the people had every right to rebel. This view resulted in Mason's own conclusion that the colonies deserved independence and a new government. Mason's fellow revolutionaries, especially Washington, admired his literary talent and his constitutional expertise. Thomas Jefferson remarked that Mason "was learned in the lore of our former Constitution," referring to the British government. Indeed, Mason had made it a point to study every Constitution that had ever existed.

Bronze of George Mason at his homestead

By 1776, Mason was wealthy, had political experience, and had demonstrated his intellectual abilities. He was a perfect choice to represent Virginia in the Continental Congress. Two-thirds of the members of the Virginia legislature appealed to him to serve in the second Continental Congress. Both Patrick Henry and Thomas Jefferson told Mason that the cause needed him. However, Mason declined to serve, saying it would be a full-time job that would take precedence over his motherless children.

The appeal to his family duty succeeded, and Mason avoided the trip to Philadelphia. Still, he himself noted that "my getting clear of this Appointment has avail'd me little." During the Revolution, he served as a member of the House of Delegates from 1776 to 1781, his longest continuous service outside Fairfax County, which he represented in Richmond. Due to an illness brought on by a botched smallpox inoculation, Mason missed a portion of the legislature's spring 1777 session. During his absence, the delegates elected him to the Continental Congress. Once again, he declined, arguing that he was needed at home and that without the permission of his constituents, he could not resign from the General Assembly.

Mason was appointed to the Annapolis Convention of 1786, but like most of the delegates, he decided not to attend. The most crucial decision made at the sparsely attended meeting was a call for a conference to consider amendments to the Articles of Confederation. This conference became the 1787 Constitutional Convention held in Philadelphia. Virginia decided that George Washington, James Madison, George Wythe, James Blair, and Mason would represent that state at the convention. Mason had never traveled outside Virginia or Maryland in his life; however, in this instance, despite his chronic ill health, he decided to make what would prove to be a difficult journey. His decision to attend surprised many as he said he "would not, upon pecuniary motives, serve in this convention for a thousand pounds per day." According to the historian Jeff Broadwater, "Mason went to Philadelphia because he believed the convention would do important work because a near consensus existed among America's political elite that Congress needed new powers and because he saw a stronger central government as a potential check on state legislatures." In *1787: The Grand Convention* by the historian Clinton Rossiter the author speculates that Mason saw the meeting as the last hope for the preservation of property-owning republicanism in the United States.

Mason impressed many of his fellow delegates. William Pierce said, "Mr. Mason is a gentleman of remarkable strong powers, and possesses a clear and copious understanding. He is able and convincing in debate and firm in his principles, and undoubtedly one of the best politicians in America," Virginia Governor Edmund Randolph observes, "Among the numbers who in their small circles were propagating with activity the American doctrines was George Mason in the shade of retirement. He extended their grasp upon the opinions and affections of those with whom he conversed. He was behind none of the sons of Virginia in knowledge of her history and interest. At a glance, he saw to the bottom of every proposition which affected her. His elocution was manly sometimes but not wantonly sarcastic.

Mason favored a more powerful central government, but not at the expense of local interests. He also worried that northern states would dominate the union and pass trade restrictions that would harm Virginia. He supported a balance of powers he viewed as necessary for a durable government. Early in the convention, Mason favored the Virginia plan, which proposed a popularly elected lower house whose members would choose the members of the upper house from lists provided by the states. The plan also called for representation in both houses to be based on population. This part of the plan was opposed by the smaller states. Mason served on a committee to address the conflict. The committee put forward what was known as the Great Compromise, whereby the House of Representatives members would be based on population in which money bills must originate. The upper house, the Senate, would have equal representation from each state.

The convention had opened in late May, and it was in the middle of July that the delegates began to move past their deadlock relative to representation relying on the framework of the Great Compromise. During these debates, Mason exerted considerable influence. He was successful in proposing a minimum age requirement of twenty-five to serve in Congress after expressing his view that younger men lacked the necessary maturity. He also put forth the proposal that the federal government not be in any state capital. On August 6, 1787, the convention received a draft of a constitution written by the Committee of Detail. Mason viewed the draft as acceptable as a starting point for debate.

In the debates that followed, Mason was successful in some of his arguments, including banning Congress from imposing an export tax and placing state militias under federal control. However, he was unsuccessful in obtaining a consensus for certain proposals he deemed necessary, such as the failure of the Constitution to include a Bill of Rights. Despite being the owner of a large number of slaves, Mason also proposed that the Constitution ban the importation of slaves. He failed to prevail as

Grave of George Mason

the convention allowed for the importation of slaves to continue until at least 1800. On August 31, 1787, Elbridge Gerry, a delegate from
Massachusetts, moved to postpone consideration of the final document,
and Mason seconded the motion, stating that "he would sooner chop off
his right hand than put it to the Constitution as it now stands."

On September 12th, the Committee on Style submitted its final
draft. On September 15th, as the convention was considering each
clause contained in the draft, three delegates, Edmund Randolph, Gerry,
and Mason, announced that they would not sign the Constitution.
Gouverneur Morris, a Pennsylvania delegate who is the principal author
of the Constitution, developed a plan to secure those last signatures.

Morris drafted the following to appear above the signatures, "Done in Convention, by the unanimous consent of the state's present . . . In witness whereof, we have hereunto subscribed our names." The language reflected that the signers agreed that the states had voted for the Constitution not that every signer agreed with it. The ploy failed. In Mason's view, the Constitution failed to protect the rights of the people, put excessive power in the hands of the federal government and would lead to some form of tyranny. He refused to put his signature on the document. In a letter to his son, John, Mason noted that his action had cost him at least one important friendship, writing, "I believe there were few men in whom (Washington) placed greater confidence; but it is possible my opposition to the new government, both as a member of the national and of the Virginia Convention, may have altered the case."

There are many who view James Madison as the "Father of the Bill of Rights" because he guided the first ten amendments to the Constitution through Congress. Those who hold this view ignore the fact that Madison opposed a Bill of Rights at both the Philadelphia convention and at the Virginia Ratifying Convention. At both gatherings, it was Mason who championed the need for the Constitution to include a Bill of Rights. Even after failing to prevail, Mason continued to push for amendments

George Mason's vault

to the Constitution, keeping the issue alive before the American public. Finally, the amendments that make up our Bill of Rights came, according to Mason's biographer, "almost verbatim from the amendments Mason wrote at the Virginia Ratifying Convention and his previous 1776 Virginia Declaration of Rights." These facts certainly support the view that it is Mason who should be regarded as the "Father of the Bill of Rights."

After losing his fight against ratification in Richmond, Mason returned to his home, where he often wrote to political figures regarding his views on the new government. In 1790, United States Senator William Grayson's death left a vacancy, and Mason was offered the position. He declined, citing health reasons, but it is worth noting that Congress required its members to take an oath to support the Constitution. The seat went to future President James Monroe.

In early October 1792, Thomas Jefferson visited Mason at Gunston Hall. He noted that while Mason remained sharp in mind, he needed a crutch to walk. Less than a week after Jefferson's visit, Mason passed away on October 7, 1792. He was laid to rest on the grounds of his estate.

Daniel Morgan
(1735/6 – 1802)

Victor at Cowpens

Buried at Mount Hebron Cemetery,
Winchester, Virginia.

———————

Military

Daniel Morgan was one of the most respected battlefield tacticians of the American Revolution, serving with George Washington, Benedict Arnold, Horatio Gates, and Nathanael Greene during most of the war's major campaigns. Morgan's Riflemen were an elite unit of sharpshooters under his leadership. Morgan was best known for his victory over Banastre Tarleton at the Battle of Cowpens in South Carolina. This served as an inspiration for the fictional character Benjamin Martin in the 2000 film *The Patriot* starring Mel Gibson.

———————

Morgan's origins have always been sketchy. He was never one to speak of it, and anyone who asked was bluntly discouraged from the inquiry. What he did tell people who came to know him is he was of Welsh stock who had emigrated to Philadelphia and settled along the Delaware River. As a young man of seventeen, circa 1752, he headed across Pennsylvania to Carlisle, where he worked a few weeks, before continuing to Winchester in the Shenandoah Valley. There he was a laborer and then a sawyer in a sawmill. He was also a teamster.

Biographers have estimated his birth year as 1735. Some link him to Pennsylvania and others to New Jersey. One biographer states Morgan

Daniel Morgan (1735/6 – 1802)

Daniel Morgan

was the fifth of seven children of James Morgan (1702–1782) and Eleanor Lloyd (1706–1748). Morgan apparently left home after a fight with his father and headed off into the wilderness. He was well-equipped for it, exhibiting all the skills needed for pioneer life. However, he was not educated and may have been illiterate.

Over two years, Morgan saved enough from his labors to purchase his own team and extra wagons. Soon, he had a thriving business. During the French and Indian War, he was a civilian teamster helping supply the British Army along with, according to one source, his cousin Daniel Boone. Morgan was a teamster in the ill-fated Braddock Expedition and survived the attack. At some point, while retreating or after, Morgan had a confrontation with a British officer who had insulted him. Morgan, ever the country tough, hauled off and punched the man, knocking him out cold. This led to the severe punishment of 500 lashes. According to Morgan, he counted the lashes and realized they had stopped one short. He decided not to point out the error as he took the punishment with a grin. The officer, seeing the apparent cheerfulness of Morgan during the beating, later apologized to him. Morgan attributed this treatment to his growing disdain for British authorities.

By the early 1760s, a local merchant noted that Morgan had three different women buying sundries on his credit. One of them was Abigail Curry, who soon moved in with him. In time, Abigail gave birth to two daughters, Nancy and Betsy. Meanwhile, Morgan served as a rifleman, protecting settlements in the wilderness of Pennsylvania and New York from Indian raiders. Outside Fort Ashby, now West Virginia, Morgan and his companion were ambushed by Indians. He was struck by a musket ball that transited the back of his neck, crushing his left jaw as it exited his cheek. He lost all his teeth on that side of his mouth but survived. He carried the scars with him for the rest of his life. Another time, he led a force that rescued Fort Edward in New York and directed its defense.

After the French and Indian War, Morgan purchased a farm in Virginia between Winchester and Battletown, now Berryville. In 1774, he served in Dunmore's War, participating in raids on Indian villages in western Pennsylvania and northern Virginia. He was made a captain in the Frederick County Militia.

As the American Revolution began in the spring of 1775, Virginia agreed to send two of the ten rifle companies requested by the Continental Congress. The Committee of Frederick County unanimously selected Morgan to form and lead one of them, dubbed Morgan's Riflemen. These men were armed with long rifles with a range of 300 yards compared to the standard musket range of only 80 yards. Morgan recruited 96 men and had them assemble on July 14, 1775, in Winchester. Hugh Stephenson raised another company in nearby Shepherdstown. They had planned to meet Morgan's company at Winchester but found them gone. On what was called the "Bee-Line March," Morgan and his men traversed 600 miles to Boston, Massachusetts, in only 21 days, arriving August 6. Stephenson and his men arrived five days later. Morgan's men, who were sharpshooters, took to the woods and began sniping British officers and soldiers, killing ten a day. This outraged the British Army. They also wore hunting shirts as part of their uniforms. This eventually struck fear in British soldiers because of the known accuracy of the riflemen wearing such shirts.

Later in 1775, Morgan was chosen to lead three rifle companies in the invasion of Canada, and he led the advance party. In the assault on Quebec, when his superior, Colonel Benedict Arnold, fell injured, Morgan took command of the assault and penetrated the city. When General Richard Montgomery fell dead, Morgan was the senior officer on the field. Despite his outstanding leadership, his forces were overrun, and he was taken captive. He handed his sword to a priest, refusing to give it to the British commander, General Guy Carleton. He remained a prisoner of war until he was exchanged in January 1777.

While Morgan was a prisoner in Canada, George Washington wrote to the Continental Congress to recommend his promotion to succeed Colonel Hugh Stephenson as the rifle unit commander. Congress then appointed Morgan to the rank of colonel in the Continental Army. When Morgan rejoined the army in early 1777, he was surprised to hear he had been promoted for his bravery in Quebec. He then raised the 11th Virginia Regiment of the Continental Line, a new unit. On June 13, 1777, Morgan took command of 500 riflemen from Virginia, Maryland, and Pennsylvania called the Provisional Rifle Corps. Washington ordered them to harass General William Howe's forces as they withdrew from Philadelphia, across New Jersey, back to New York. Morgan and his men disguised themselves as Indians and used guerilla maneuvers against the British.

In September 1777, some of Morgan's regiment, including Morgan, was assigned to Horatio Gates for the Saratoga campaign. Morgan and his riflemen were instrumental in Burgoyne's surrender there. At Freeman's Farm on September 19, Morgan's men ran into the advance wing of Burgoyne's force. In the initial volley, all the British officers in the advance party were killed, and the British retreated. As the British force returned to the field, the two sides fought to a stalemate.

On October 7 at Bemis Heights, one of Morgan's riflemen killed British General Simon Fraser at the urging of Benedict Arnold. This helped to turn the tide of the battle. Arnold and Morgan then turned a counterattack from Burgoyne. That night, Burgoyne withdrew to the village of Saratoga, New York (now Schuylerville). As Burgoyne's forces dug in over the following week, Morgan's men harassed British patrols,

convincing them further retreat was not possible. Burgoyne then surrendered. Gates heaped praise on Morgan and his unit. Morgan is depicted in the painting by John Trumbull entitled *The Surrender of General
Burgoyne.*

After Saratoga, throughout 1778, Morgan was in New Jersey with
Washington, harassing British supply lines. He was not at the Battle of
Monmouth and did not receive an expected promotion to brigadier general. Instead, he was made colonel of the 7th Virginia Regiment, a lateral
move, likely due to his lack of political connections in the Congress.
Citing his aggravated legs and back from the abuse he took in Quebec,
the frustrated Morgan accepted an "honorable furlough" to resign from
the army in early 1779.

General Gates, who had taken command of the Southern Department,
called up Morgan to return to the army in June 1780. Morgan saw that
an opportunity for higher command was not on the table and declined
the offer. When Gates then suffered a resounding defeat at Camden,
South Carolina, Morgan reconsidered and joined Gates at Hillsborough,
North Carolina. There, he supported the state militias until Congress
elevated him to brigadier general in November.

Nathanael Greene then assumed command of southern American
troops. He met with Morgan on December 3, 1780, at Charlotte, North
Carolina, and granted Morgan command over a portion of his forces.
They were tasked with harassing the enemy in the South Carolina backcountry while avoiding direct conflict. British General Cornwallis then
sent Colonel Banastre Tarleton and his legion to track down Morgan.
Learning of this, Morgan disobeyed Greene and decided to rally the militia to attack.

On January 17, 1781, the two forces met at Cowpens, South Carolina.
Along with militia under Andrew Pickens and dragoons under William
Washington, Morgan confronted a superior force of Tarleton's Legion,
supplemented by other troops. Morgan took advantage of Tarleton's disdain for the militia and his riflemen's accuracy to lure the British into a
trap. As Tarleton's forces advanced confidently, believing they were attacking militia firing and retreating, they were subject to the bullets from
the sharpshooters. In less than an hour, over ninety percent of the British

troops were killed, wounded, or captured as well as all their supplies and equipment. Tarleton managed to escape with a small number of troops. Morgan's plan was considered a tactical masterpiece and touted as one of the most successfully executed double envelopes (attacks on both flanks) in all modern warfare. This turned the tide of the war in the South.

Back in Virginia, the commonwealth granted him a forfeited Tory estate. Given the constant pain of his sciatica during the damp, chilly campaign, Morgan returned to Virginia on February 10, 1781. He was back on the field briefly that July pursuing Tarleton with Lafayette, but the Legionnaire escaped. Three months later, at Yorktown, Washington found Cornwallis significantly weakened thanks to Morgan's victory.

Morgan settled into land investing. He accumulated an estate of over 250,000 acres. In 1782, he built a house near Winchester dubbed Saratoga using Hessian labor. In 1790, Congress awarded him a gold medal commemorating his victory at Cowpens.

President Washington called him out of retirement in 1794 to assist General "Light-Horse Harry" Lee with suppressing the Whiskey Rebellion in western Pennsylvania. At this point, he was promoted to major general. The massive show of force helped to end the rebellion without a shot fired. Morgan, who lost his run for the US House of Representatives, remained until 1795, commanding the remnant of the army that stayed to enforce the peace. Among them was Meriwether Lewis.

In 1796, Morgan ran again for the US House of Representatives and won seventy percent of the vote. He was a Federalist, defeating the Democratic-Republican Robert Rutherford. Morgan held the seat for one term until early 1799, retiring due to his declining health. A doctor who was attending Morgan noticed the welts on his back from his punishment in his youth. Morgan's body was battered from his many engagements. Morgan died at his daughter's home in Winchester on July 6, 1802. He was buried at the Old Stone Presbyterian Church but was later moved to Mount Hebron Cemetery in Winchester after the Civil War. Wife Abigail followed him into the grave in 1816. She is buried in Logan County, Kentucky.

Numerous states have counties named in his honor. Morganton, North Carolina, and Morganfield, Kentucky, are named after him, as are numerous squares, streets, and schools. Likewise, many statues of Morgan have been erected. Confederate General John Hunt Morgan claimed to be a descendant.

An attempt was made in 1951 to reinter Morgan's body at Cowpens, South Carolina, but the Frederick-Winchester Historical Society blocked this. In 1973, his home Saratoga became a National Historic Landmark. In 2000, Morgan was the basis for the character Benjamin Martin in the movie *The Patriot*.

Memorial to Daniel Morgan.

Thomas Nelson Jr.
(1738 – 1789)

The Governor Who Was All-In

Buried at Grace Episcopal Churchyard,
Yorktown, Virginia.

———•◆•———

Declaration of Independence • Military

Thomas Nelson Jr. was a wealthy planter, soldier, and statesman who served many terms in the colonial Virginia General Assembly and in the Continental Congress, where he signed the Declaration of Independence. He was governor of Virginia in 1781 and fought in the militia during the Siege of Yorktown. He used his assets to prop up Virginia and the state militia during the American Revolution, only to see his property destroyed by the British and his fortune ruined.

———◆•◆———

Thomas Nelson Jr. was born December 26, 1738, in Yorktown, Virginia, the oldest son of William Nelson Sr. and his wife, Elizabeth (née Burwell). The elder Nelson served twice as the royal governor of Virginia in 1770 and 1771. Nelson's maternal grandfather, Robert "King" Carter, was one of the wealthiest Virginians and a royal governor. On his father's side, Nelson was the grandson of Thomas "Scotch Tom" Nelson, an early pioneer at Yorktown who emigrated from Cumberland, England. One genealogist stated these Nelsons were distant relations of Lord Horatio Nelson.

Nelson was tagged as a junior due to his uncle by the same name. He attended private schools in Virginia before heading to England to

Thomas Nelson Jr.

study at Hackney, near London. He then attended Christ's College at Cambridge University in May 1758. He graduated in 1760 and returned to Virginia the following year. In 1762 Nelson married Lucy Grymes, a wealthy widow, with whom he eventually had eleven children, including Hugh Nelson, who served in the US House of Representatives from 1811 to 1823. Grymes's first husband was Carter Burwell, and she was the niece of Peyton Randolph, who was a brother-in-law of Benjamin Harrison V. Grimes's aunt was the mother of "Light-Horse Harry" Lee.

Nelson was primarily a planter, helping his father manage his various plantations and the estates owned by his two minor stepsons. He also entered politics and was first elected by York County voters to the Virginia House of Burgesses in 1761, replacing Robert Carter Nicholas. He served six more terms and was also on His Majesty's Council in 1764.

By 1774, after the Stamp and Sugar Acts, Nelson turned against the Crown. At Williamsburg on March 20, 1775, Nelson voted for the measure proposed by Patrick Henry to arm Virginians to fight the British. It was Nelson who introduced a resolution in the Virginia House to declare independence from England. As tensions with the mother country escalated, Nelson was appointed a colonel in the militia's 2nd Virginia Regiment. On August 11, 1775, before Nelson could become engaged in the military, he was elected as a member of the Virginia delegation to the Continental Congress.

Nelson arrived to attend the opening of the Continental Congress on September 11, 1775. According to the diary of John Adams, "Thomas Nelson, Esq., George Wythe, Esq., and Francis Lightfoot Lee, Esq., appeared as delegates from Virginia. Nelson is a fat man, like the late Colonel Lee of Marblehead. He is a speaker, and alert and lively for his weight." Nelson served through February 23, 1776, when he returned home. There, he attended Virginia's constitutional convention that spring.

Nelson returned to the Continental Congress on June 9, 1776. He was one of thirteen members appointed to the committee on June 12 to begin work on what ultimately became the Articles of Confederation. In July, Nelson voted for independence from England and signed the Declaration to that effect. Nelson served in the Congress until May 8, 1777, traveling back and forth from Virginia. During this time, Nelson was appointed a brigadier general and the commander-in-chief of all of Virginia's forces in the Continental Army. Nelson took command and raised an army. He marched them to Philadelphia, which had been invaded by the British. However, Congress was unable to pay the troops and ordered them disbanded.

On December 10, 1778, Nelson was again appointed to the Continental Congress, serving from February 18 to April 22, 1779. Due to a bout of illness, he returned to Virginia, where he financed the state's activities and the militia, acting as the commander-in-chief. By 1781, Nelson succeeded Thomas Jefferson, following William Fleming's nine days as acting governor). During this time, the British invaded Virginia and took Nelson's home, Nelson House, as a headquarters for Cornwallis.

Wrote a descendant, Channing Moon Thompson, in 1898, "In June 1781 [Nelson] was chosen Governor of [the] State of Virginia & took part in the siege of Yorktown as Major General in the American Army. His force of 3000 men was raised and equipped at his own expense. At the time of the siege, his own house was his headquarters, & later, during an engagement, he ordered it to be fired into, saying to General Lafayette 'Spare no particle of my property so long as it affords comfort or shelter to the enemies of my country.'" According to another source, Nelson offered five guineas to the first man to hit his house.

Though victorious at Yorktown, Nelson was under a tremendous financial strain, having utilized much of his personal and family fortune in sustaining the state and the army. He was now in debt. Despite these issues, Nelson continued as a member of the Virginia House of Delegates, representing York County through 1788. Thomas Nelson Jr. died at his son's home in Hanover County, Virginia, on January 4, 1789, and was buried at the Grace Episcopal Churchyard in Yorktown. Wrote Colonel James Innes in tribute:

> The illustrious General Thomas Nelson is no more! He paid the last great debt to nature, on Sunday, the fourth of the present month, at his estate in Hanover. He who undertakes barely to recite the exalted virtues which adorned the life of this great and good man, will unavoidably pronounce a panegyric on human nature. As a man, a citizen, a legislator, and a patriot, he exhibited a conduct untarnished and undebased by sordid or selfish interest, and strongly marked with the genuine characteristics of true religion, sound benevolence, and liberal policy. Entertaining the most ardent love for civil and religious liberty, he was among the first of that glorious band of patriots whose exertions dashed and defeated the machinations of British tyranny and gave United America freedom and independent empire. At a most important crisis, during the late struggle for American liberty, when this state appeared to be designated as the theatre of action for the contending armies, he was selected by the unanimous suffrage of the legislature to command the virtuous yeomanry of his country; in this honourable

employment he remained until the end of the war; as a soldier, he was indefatigably active and coolly intrepid; resolute and un-dejected in misfortunes, he towered above distress, and struggled with the manifold difficulties to which his situation exposed him, with constancy and courage. In the memorable year 1781, when the whole force of the southern British army was directed to the immediate subjugation of this state, he was called to the helm of government; this was a juncture which indeed 'tried men's souls.'

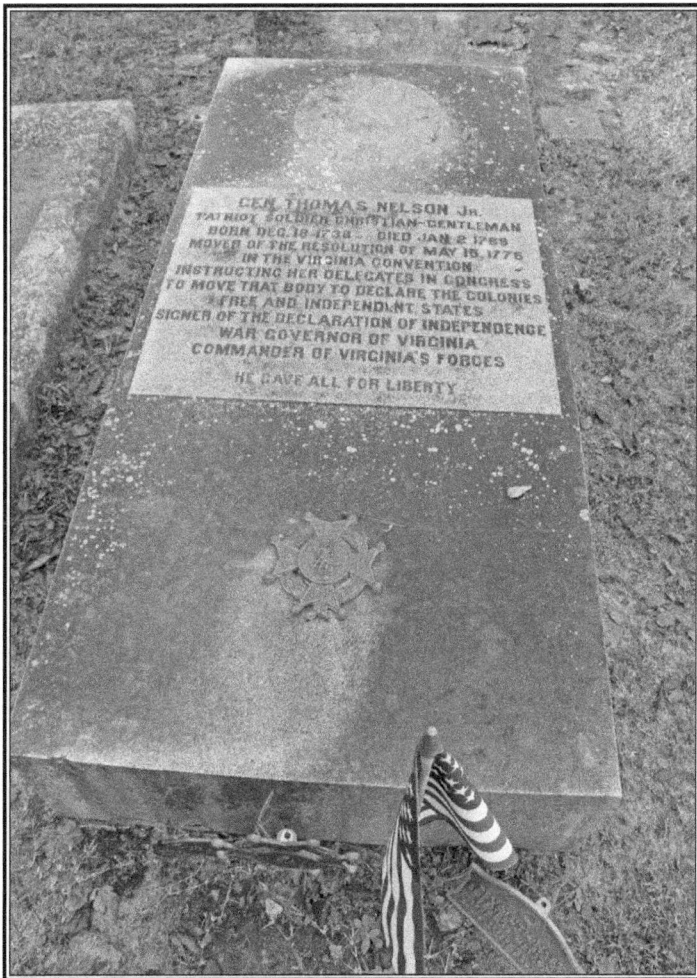

The grave of Thomas Nelson Jr.

He did not avail himself of this opportunity to retire in the rear of danger; but on the contrary, took the field at the head of his countrymen; and at the hazard of his life, his fame, and individual fortune, by his decision and magnanimity, he saved not only his country, but all America, from disgrace, if not from total ruin. Of this truly patriotic and heroic conduct, the renowned commander in chief, with all the gallant officers of the combined armies employed at the siege of York, will bear ample testimony; this part of his conduct even contemporary jealousy, envy, and malignity were forced to approve, and this, more impartial posterity, if it can believe, will almost adore. If, after contemplating the splendid and heroic parts of his character, we shall inquire for the milder virtues of humanity, and seek for the man, we shall find the refined, beneficent, and social qualities of private life, through all its forms and combinations, so happily modified and united in him, that in the words of the darling poet of nature, it may be said: His life was gentle: and the elements so mixed in him, that nature might stand up And say to all the world—this was a man.

Nelson House, in Yorktown, Virginia, is a National Historic Landmark maintained by the US National Park Service at the Colonial National Historical Park. Nelson Counties in Virginia and Kentucky are named in his honor, as is the Thomas Nelson Community College and the Thomas Nelson High School.

Edmund Pendleton
(1721 – 1803)

"Here Comes the Judge!"

Buried in the Bruton Parish Church Sanctuary,
Williamsburg, Virginia.

———•—•———

Continental Association

Edmund Pendleton was a long-time member of the Virginia House of Burgesses in colonial times who was also the speaker of that body. He was elected to the First Continental Congress, famously riding on horseback from Mount Vernon, Virginia, to Philadelphia with George Washington and Patrick Henry. There, Pendleton signed the Continental Association. He later contributed resolutions for the Declaration of Independence in the Virginia Assembly, some of the ideas which Thomas Jefferson incorporated. Pendleton then served many years as a judge in Virginia, including in the state supreme court. He was the uncle of fellow Continental Congress delegates Nathaniel Pendleton and John Penn, a signer of the Declaration.

———•—•———

Edmund Pendleton was born on September 9, 1721, in Caroline County, Virginia, the seventh child of Henry Pendleton and his wife, Mary Bishop (née Taylor) Pendleton. Henry's grandfather, also named Henry, emigrated from Norwich, England, in the late 1600s. Henry Pendleton never got to see baby Edmund as he died four months before his son's birth. James Taylor, Mary's father, was a plantation owner in

Edmund Pendleton

Rappahannock County who helped the widow and her children until she married Edward Watkins in 1723.

The Watkins stepchildren grew up under meager circumstances. At 14, young Edmund became apprenticed to Colonel Benjamin Robinson, the Clerk of the Caroline Court. Pendleton became exposed to politics and the law. He began reading law books and learning legal procedures. In 1737, at 16, he became the Clerk of the Vestry of St. Mary's Parish in Caroline. He used the money he made to purchase law books and read them diligently. By 1741, at 20, Pendleton was licensed as an attorney. On January 21, 1741, he married Elizabeth Roy, but she died in childbirth on November 16, 1742. The infant son did not survive. On June 20, 1743, Pendleton married Sarah Pollard, the daughter of Joseph and Priscilla Pollard. The couple had no children.

Pendleton worked first in county courts and then as the prosecuting attorney for Essex County. This allowed him to join the general court bar in October 1745. He then accepted an appointment to justice of the peace for Caroline County in 1751. Pendleton trained his nephews,

John Penn (a future signed of the Declaration of Independence) and John Taylor (a future U.S. Senator). From 1752 until 1776, Pendleton represented Caroline County in the Virginia House of Burgesses until dissolved at the outset of the American Revolution.

When the Stamp Act was enacted and the distributor of the stamps resigned, Pendleton encouraged as much legal activity as possible without using stamps, such as recording wills. In 1766, when his mentor, John Robinson, who was speaker of the House of Burgesses, died, Pendleton was appointed one of the executors. He helped uncover a scandal involving Robinson's incredible debt, who was assumed to be very wealthy. This controversy lasted for over forty years until it was settled.

As tensions arose with England, Pendleton was on the Virginia Committee of Correspondence in 1773. In August 1774, he attended the convention in Williamsburg to choose delegates to the First Continental Congress. The following delegates were selected from Virginia: Peyton Randolph, Richard Henry Lee, George Washington, Patrick Henry, Richard Bland, Benjamin Harrison, and Edmund Pendleton. He then rode to Philadelphia on horseback with Patrick Henry and George Washington. There, on October 14, 1774, he signed the Continental Association. The following year, on July 8, he signed the Olive Branch Petition. Around that time, in the Second Continental Congress, he proposed a resolution stating, "The ground and foundation of the present unhappy dispute between the British Ministry and Parliament and America, is a Right claimed by the former to tax the Subjects of the latter without their consent, and not an inclination on our part to set up for independency, which we utterly disavow and wish to restore to a Constitutional Connection upon the most solid and reasonable basis."

Back in Williamsburg on December 1, 1775, Pendleton, as President of the Committee of Safety, was president of the convention held to discuss Virginia's disposition. During the convention, there was a call to draft a declaration of independence from England. They asked that all the colonies adopt it. It was the first such declaration in the colonies. The convention also debated George Mason's Virginia Declaration of Rights, which later served as a model for the Declaration of Independence. Pendleton won the support of slave owners for the measure by suggesting that universal rights exclude slaves.

On May 6, 1776, another convention was called in Williamsburg, and Pendleton was again elected the president. Pendleton addressed the convention: "We are now met in General Convention according to the ordinance for our election, at a time truly critical, when the subjects of the most important and interesting nature require our serious attention. The administration of justice, and almost all the powers of government, have now been suspended for near two years. It will become us to reflect whether we can longer sustain the great struggle we are making in this situation; and the case of criminals confined and not tried, and others who may be apprehended pursuant to our laws, deserves particular notice. Our military and naval arrangements, as well as the funds for supporting them, will call for our revision; and the ordinance prescribing a mode of punishment for the enemies of America in this colony being very defective, will require amendment . . ."

That November, Pendleton, Thomas Jefferson, George Wythe, George Mason, and Thomas Ludwell Lee were appointed to a committee to revise Virginia's laws. Pendleton was also elected as the speaker of the Virginia House of Delegates, the new state legislature. In March 1777, Pendleton fell from his horse and dislocated his hip. This forced him to use crutches for the rest of his life. That year he became a judge of the High Court of Chancery. The following year, he was appointed the president of the Virginia Supreme Court of Appeal, a position he held until his death.

In 1788, Pendleton was unanimously elected president of the Virginia Ratifying Convention for the U.S. Constitution by the 168 delegates. After days of debate open to the public, the Constitution narrowly passed, making Virginia the tenth state to ratify it. Pendleton and his friend George Wythe voted in favor. Friend Patrick Henry was opposed. Of primary concern was the addition of a Bill of Rights proposed by George Mason and sponsored by James Madison.

On October 23, 1803, Judge Edmund Pendleton died at his 2300-acre estate "Edmundsbury" near Bowling Green, Virginia. He was initially buried on the grounds of the estate. Due to his former estate's decay in 1907, his remains were exhumed and reinterred within Bruton Parish Episcopal Church in Williamsburg, Virginia. The slab covering his tomb says simply, "Edmund Pendleton of Caroline."

Pendleton left no descendants. His nephew, the son of his brother John, was named Edmund Pendleton, Jr., and became the principal heir. His nephew Nathaniel Pendleton, Jr., distinguished himself as an aide to General Nathanael Greene. Many Pendletons in succeeding generations became judges in Virginia. A relative, Philip Pendleton Barbour, served on the U.S. Supreme Court and as Speaker of the House. James Barbour, Philip's brother, served as governor of Virginia, in the U.S. Senate, and as secretary of war. Other Pendleton relations served in the military, including for the Confederacy during the Civil War.

Pendleton counties in West Virginia and Kentucky are named in honor of Edmund Pendleton.

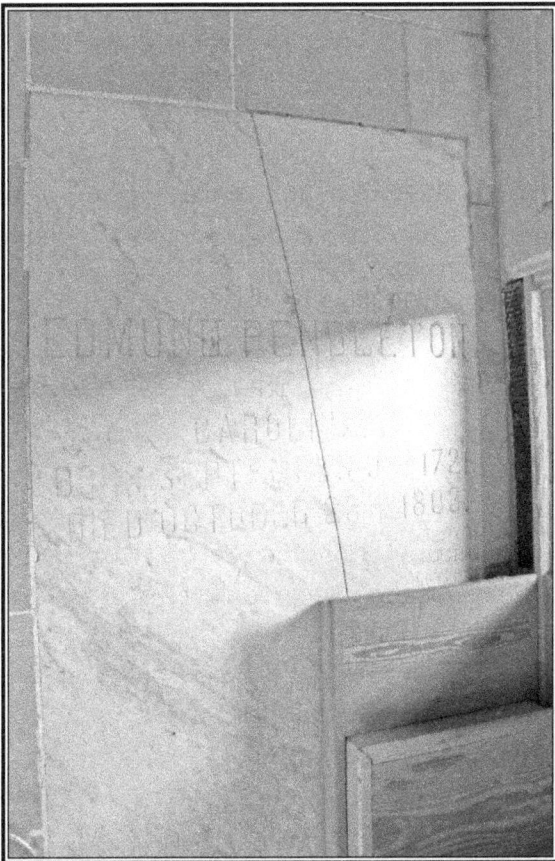

The tomb of Edmund Pendleton.

Edmund Randolph
(1753–1813)

Jefferson's Chameleon

Buried at Old Chapel Cemetery,
Millwood, Virginia.

———————

**Military • Continental Congress • Constitutional Convention
Attorney General • Secretary of State**

This founder was born into an influential Virginia family. Benjamin Harrison, who would become the father and great grandfather of two American presidents, considered him "one of the cleverest young men in America." He studied the law and became one of the country's most respected lawyers. His parents remained loyal to the crown, and as the trouble between England and the colonies grew, they returned to the mother country. He served in the Continental Army and represented Virginia in the Continental Congress. After the Revolution, he became the seventh governor of Virginia. He also served as a delegate to the 1787 Constitutional Convention, where he played an influential role but was one of the three members who refused to sign the finished product. President Washington selected him to be the nation's first attorney general. He also served as Secretary of State but was forced to resign from that office because Washington was led to believe that he had revealed sensitive information to France. In 1807 he was part of the defense team that successfully defended former Vice President Aaron Burr in his treason trial. His name was Edmund Randolph.

Edmund Randolph

Randolph was born in Williamsburg, Virginia, on August 10, 1753. The Randolph's were considered one of the colony's most prominent families of lawyers-statesmen. He received his education at the College of William and Mary and then studied the law at the office of his father, John Randolph, and his uncle, Peyton Randolph. When the American Revolution began in 1775, his loyalist parents returned to England. Their son decided on a different route joining the Continental Army, where he served as an aide-de-camp to General George Washington. In October 1775, his uncle Peyton passed away, and he left the army, returning to Virginia to assume the role of executor of the estate.

In 1776 Randolph served as the youngest delegate to the Virginia Convention that wrote the state's constitution. In August of that year, he married Elizabeth Nicholas, the daughter of Robert Carter Nicholas, Virginia's state treasurer. The couple would have six children, including Peyton Randolph, who would become governor of Virginia in 1811.

Randolph was then elected the Mayor of Williamsburg and became his state's first attorney general. In 1779 he was selected to be one of Virginia's eleven delegates in the Continental Congress. He served in Congress until 1782 and, during this time, maintained a private law practice where he handled numerous legal issues for many noted Patriots, including George Washington. According to Michael Klarman in his book *The Framers Coup,* his contemporaries considered Randolph "one of the most distinguished men in America by his talents and his influence" and as "a young gentleman in whom unite all the accomplishments of the scholar and the statesmen." Enough Virginians shared this view of Randolph to elect him to the governorship of the state in 1786. At this point, he turned his lucrative law practice over to future Supreme Court Chief Justice John Marshall because Virginia law prohibited executive officers from practicing law in the state courts.

In 1787 at the age of 34, Randolph traveled to Philadelphia as a member of the Virginia delegation to attend the Constitutional Convention. As reported by James Madison, Randolph addressed the issue facing the convention, "The true question is whether we shall adhere to the federal plan or introduce the national plan. The insufficiency of the former has been fully displayed by the trial already made . . . A national government alone, properly constituted, will answer the purpose, and he begged it to be considered that the present is the last moment for establishing one. After this select experiment, the people will yield to despair."

Fifty-five delegates attended the convention, which worked from May 29 until September 17, 1787, the day of the signing. Of the delegates, 29 were recorded as having attended every session. The historian Clinton Rossiter in his work *1787: The Grand Convention,* described these 29 as "full-timers." Randolph was one of the full-timers, as was his good friend James Madison. Randolph introduced the idea, for which Madison was mainly responsible, known as the "Virginia Plan." In introducing the plan, Randolph presented it as a response to the deficiencies in the Articles of Confederation. However, he took pains not to criticize the Articles' creators themselves, calling them "wise and great men" who were limited by "the jealousy of the states regarding their sovereignty." The plan Randolph introduced was an outline for a new national government. In his aforementioned work, Michael Klarman stated that the plan and its resolutions "became the convention's first substantive business and would remain its focal point for its duration."

Throughout the convention, Randolph was an active participant in the various debates on the issues raised by the delegates. In his work, the historian Rossiter counts Randolph among a group of attendees that he calls the influentials. Rossiter and other historians give Randolph "considerable credit for the decision to enumerate the powers of Congress." Given the above, one would have expected Randolph to be a supporter of the convention's finished product. This, however, was not the case. Before the vote on the Constitution was taken, Benjamin Franklin urged all present to add their signature to the document. Franklin professed his high regard for Randolph, who had already made it clear that he was unlikely to sign. Randolph motioned that state conventions be permitted to offer amendments to the proposed Constitution and that a second convention be held to act on the state's proposals. Randolph added that if his proposition were not adopted, it would be impossible for him to put his name on the document. Every state voted no on Randolph's motion, and he became one of three delegates who refused to sign the Constitution.

After returning to Virginia, Randolph published a letter explaining his opposition to the Constitution. His chief objections were the provision for equal state representation in the Senate and the absence of a supermajority requirement for commercial legislation. Despite his concerns, he concluded the letter by stating the need for "the establishment of a firm, energetic government." He added that "the most inveterate curse which can befall us is a dissolution of the Union." He stated that if the amendments he favored could not be obtained, he would accept the Constitution as it was written. In 1788 Randolph chaired the Virginia Ratifying Convention, where he supported the ratification of the Constitution. Years later, Thomas Jefferson, who was Randolph's second cousin, offered a less than positive assessment of Randolph's performance calling him, "the poorest chameleon I ever saw, having no color of his own, and reflecting that nearest him."

It appears that President Washington did not share Jefferson's view since when he formed his initial cabinet, he appointed Randolph as the first United States Attorney General. Then when Jefferson resigned as Secretary of State in 1793, Washington replaced him with Randolph. In his new role, he opposed the 1794 appointment of John Jay as the special envoy to England. Jay then negotiated a controversial treaty with Great Britain that Randolph also opposed. In 1795 Washington forced Randolph to resign based on his belief that his secretary of state had shared sensitive information with France. Randolph steadfastly maintained his innocence but recognizing that he had lost the president's

The grave of Edmund Randolph.

confidence, he left office. Modern historians have exonerated Randolph of any misconduct. After his resignation, Randolph was held responsible for $49,000 lost by the State Department during his administration, and he subsequently paid that amount.

Returning to Virginia, he resumed his law practice. His most famous client was former Vice President Aaron Burr. There is little doubt that Randolph's cousin and then-President, Thomas Jefferson, was none too pleased with the successful defense of Burr in his 1807 treason trial.

Randolph had paralysis in his final years, and he passed away at the age of 60 on September 12, 1813. He was laid to rest in the Old Chapel Cemetery in Millwood, Virginia.

The Edmund J. Randolph Award was named in his honor. It is the highest award presented by the United States Department of Justice. It is awarded to persons who make "outstanding contributions to the accomplishments of the Department's mission."

Peyton Randolph
(1721 – 1775)

The First President

Buried at Wren Chapel at the College of William and Mary,
Williamsburg, Virginia

Continental Association

Peyton Randolph was the Attorney General and Speaker of the House
of Burgesses in colonial Virginia prior to the American Revolution. He
was early to the Patriot cause despite his connections to the colonial
government. He was elected to both the First and Second Continental
Congresses and served as the first President of those bodies. As such, he
signed the Continental Association.

Randolph, born on September 10, 1721, at Tazewell Hall in
Williamsburg, Virginia, the son of Sir John Randolph and his wife,
Susannah (née Beverly or Beverley) Randolph. The Randolphs were
wealthy plantation owners, and Sir John was a barrister who also served
as Speaker of the House of Burgesses from 1734 to 1736 and as the
Virginia colony's Attorney General. Sir John's father had also been the
Speaker of the House, and the family had a long history of public ser-
vice back to Sir Thomas Randolph (1523–1590), who was an advisor to
Queen Elizabeth I.

Randolph had two brothers and one sister. The eldest brother,
Beverley Randolph (1719–1764), married Agatha Wormeley (1721–
1786) in 1742. Sister Mary Randolph (1720–1768) married Colonel

Peyton Randolph

Philip Ludwell Grymes (1721–1761), a member of the Virginia House of Burgesses, in 1742. The younger brother, John Randolph (1727–1784), married Ariana Jennings in 1750.

Sir John died in 1736, when Randolph was only 15, leaving the four children with their widowed mother. Soon after, Randolph attended the College of William and Mary in Williamsburg but did not graduate. In late 1739, he traveled to England to study law at the Middle Temple of Gray's Inn, a prominent law school. On February 10, 1744, after completing his studies, he was accepted by the London bar.

Randolph returned to Virginia and, in 1746, married Elizabeth Harrison of the Berkeley plantation, the sister of Benjamin Harrison, who would later sign the Declaration of Independence and be the grandfather and great-great-grandfather of two presidents. Peyton and Elizabeth had no children and lived on Nicholson Street in Williamsburg.

Based on a recommendation of John Hanbury, an English friend, Randolph was appointed the Attorney General for Virginia in 1748, despite the reservations of Royal Governor William Gooch. Randolph was also elected to the House of Burgesses.

In 1753, Randolph became embroiled in a dispute with Royal Governor Robert Dinwiddie when he was asked by the House of Burgesses to travel to England at the government's expense, including his salary, to oppose a land patent fee imposed by the governor before the British Board of Trade. The fee would be charged to colonists wishing to expand their land holdings. Normally, as Attorney General, Randolph was to represent the governor rather than the legislature. The governor and his council were outraged and replaced Randolph with George Wythe. Randolph arrived in London near the end of 1754 but was unable to sway the Board. However, when Randolph returned in a few months, the governor reinstated him, and the fee was dropped. This was an early instance of the colonists protesting taxation from overseas.

Following Braddock's defeat in 1755, Randolph led the "Associators," 300 militiamen who rallied to defend Virginia. On May 3, 1756, he wrote Colonel George Washington:

> Some public-spirited Gentlemen have done me the honor to fix upon me as their leader till we can come to the place where you command, when we shall be very glad to follow such orders, as you shall think most conducive to the public good.

After the French and Indian War in 1765, when Parliament was attempting to recoup the cost of the war from the colonists via the Stamp Act, the Virginia House of Burgesses selected Randolph to draft a petition to the King opposing it. Patrick Henry had raised his own objections to the Act, and most of them were accepted, superseding Randolph's more conservative petition. The amended petition was ignored by the King, and the tax was imposed.

This roiling of the colonial powers put Randolph in a position of disfavor with the governor. As he became Speaker of the House in 1766 following the death of John Robinson, he resigned from the Attorney General position and was replaced by his brother John, a Loyalist. Randolph then focused on his role in the House of Burgesses, leading a committee to collect and revise the laws of the colony in 1769. Said Thomas Jefferson of Randolph's performance as Speaker:

Altho' not eloquent, his matter was so substantial that no man commanded more attention; which, joined with a sense of his great worth gave him a weight in the House of Burgesses which few ever attained.

In reaction to the discontent regarding the Townshend Acts (1767), Governor Lord Botetourt dissolved the House of Burgesses on May 17, 1769. Randolph and other members walked to Raleigh Tavern and formed an Association, which ultimately led to non-importation agreements and boycotts of English goods. Randolph led this opposition and also issued a statement of support for the Boston Port Act in 1773 as chair of the new Committee of Correspondence.

On September 5, 1774, Randolph, George Washington, Benjamin Harrison, Edmund Pendleton, Richard Henry Lee, Patrick Henry, and Richard Bland were sent to Philadelphia as delegates to the First Continental Congress. Randolph was nominated to the President of the Congress and was unanimously approved. The Congress asked for the repeal of the Coercive Acts and signed the Continental Association. Randolph then resigned as President, to head back to Virginia. He was replaced by Henry Middleton after a term of forty-seven days.

Following Patrick Henry's "give me liberty or give me death" speech in March 1775, at which Randolph presided, Royal Governor Lord Dunmore had the Royal Marines remove the gunpowder and muskets from the armory in Williamsburg on April 21, 1775. Unknown to anyone at the time, the first shots had been fired at Lexington and Concord. Randolph and the Associators were angered by this, and Patrick Henry threatened a military response. Carter Braxton helped to negotiate a payment for the arms from the governor to avoid a confrontation.

The Second Continental Congress was called on May 10, 1775, and Randolph was once again elected its President. However, in June, when Lord Dunmore called the House of Burgesses back in session, Randolph resigned from Congress and headed home. Thomas Jefferson took his seat in Congress, and John Hancock became President. As the Speaker of the Virginia House, Randolph rejected the offer of reconciliation from Lord North, who was trying to divide the colonies by reconciling with them individually. The Continental Congress rejected it as well. As Lord

The crypt under the Wren Chapel at the College of William and Mary
containing the grave of Peyton Randolph.

Dunmore fled that June, Randolph led the formation of a Committee
of Safety.

When the Continental Congress met again in Philadelphia in
September 1775, Randolph returned as a delegate despite being in ill
health. John Adams was concerned that Randolph might want his seat
back as President when he wrote that Randolph "Sits very humbly in his
Seat, while our new [President] continues in the Chair, without Seeming
to feel the Impropriety." On October 22, 1775, while dining with
Thomas Jefferson, Randolph suffered a five-hour-long "fit of apoplexy"
and died. Said one Philadelphia newspaper (likely Franklin's):

> Last Sunday died of an apoplectic stroke, in the fifty-third year
> of his age, the Hon. Peyton Randolph, Esq; of Virginia, late
> President of the Continental Congress, a general who possessed
> the virtues of humanity in an eminent degree, and joining with
> them the soundest judgment, was the delight of his friends in

The approximate location in the Wren Chapel
under which is Randolph's crypt.

private life, and a most valuable member of society, having long
sided, and with great . . . integrity discharged the most honour-
able public trusts.

The entire Congress attended his funeral in Philadelphia on October
24, 1775. Carter Braxton was then called as a replacement for the Virginia
delegation in Congress. Randolph's body was returned to Williamsburg
and buried in the vault beneath the chapel at the College of William
and Mary. When he died, in addition to his house in Williamsburg,
Randolph also owned several pieces of land in town, two plantations in
James City County, and more than 100 slaves.

In honor of Randolph, the Congress named one of the first naval frigates the USS *Randolph* and a fort on the Ohio River as Fort Randolph. Randolph County, North Carolina; Randolph, Massachusetts; and Randolph County, Indiana, were named to his honor. During World War II, the aircraft carrier USS *Randolph* was named for him. The Peyton Randolph House in Colonial Williamsburg was declared a National Historic Landmark in 1970.

In October 1859, there was a fire in the chapel area of the college. Randolph's was the only vault damaged, but the newspaper reported his coffin was in excellent condition.

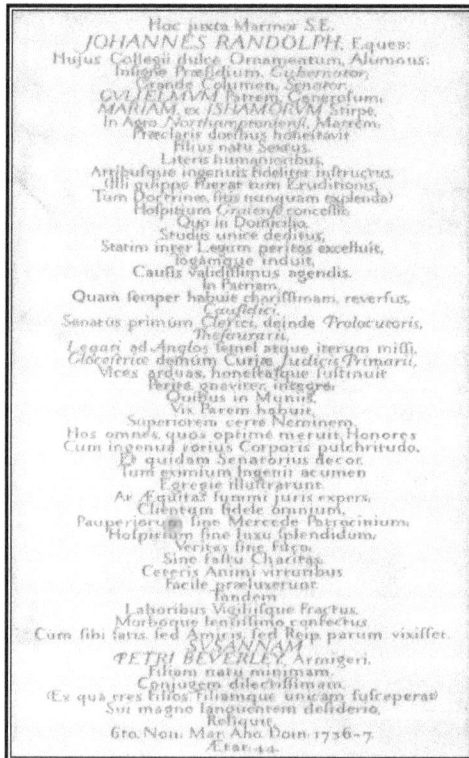

The memorial plaque in the Wren Chapel dedicated
to the Randolphs.

Daniel Roberdeau
(1727 – 1795)

Pennsylvania Associator

Buried at Hebron Cemetery.
Winchester, Virginia.

—————

Articles of Confederation • Military

Daniel Roberdeau was a Philadelphia merchant and brigadier general who led the Pennsylvania Associators, a branch of the militia. He was also a political leader in Philadelphia who was elected to the Second Continental Congress, where he signed the Articles of Confederation as a Pennsylvania delegate.

—————

Roberdeau was born in 1727 on the Island of St. Chrisopher, also known as St. Kitts, in the West Indies, east of Puerto Rico. He was the son of a French Huguenot father, Isaac Roberdeau, and his wife, Mary (née Cunningham) Roberdeau, of Scottish origin. When his father died, the family moved to Philadelphia.

Roberdeau was initially educated in England, but then learned the merchant trade in Philadelphia, where he became a timber merchant, leveraging his connections in the Caribbean.

Circa 1749 to 1754, as an early adherent of Freemasonry in Philadelphia, Roberdeau became established among the leadership of that colonial city, including Benjamin Franklin. He was elected as a city warden in 1756 and served on the hospital board with Franklin. He was then elected to the Pennsylvania Assembly from 1756 to 1760.

Daniel Roberdeau

On October 3, 1761, Roberdeau married Mary Bostwick of Philadelphia and joined in her Presbyterian faith. The couple ultimately had nine children, and Roberdeau became an elder of the church. He was again elected to the Pennsylvania Assembly, serving from 1766 to 1776, serving on the Committee of Finance and actively engaging the negotiations with the Native Americans.

Despite being involved in importing and exporting goods, Roberdeau was in favor of the non-importation protests of the early 1770s. After railing for the replacement of the current members of the Pennsylvania delegation in the Continental Congress, Roberdeau was appointed to the Pennsylvania Council of Safety in 1775 and chaired a protest against the king in May 1776 in Philadelphia that caught the attention of John Adams, who was attending the Continental Congress. Roberdeau signed as chairman of the committee that declared the King a mortal enemy.

Adams wrote to James Warren on May 20, 1776, about the event, noting how orderly it was run. Roberdeau was a staunch supporter of independence and was appointed as a brigadier general in the Pennsylvania Militia, in charge of the Pennsylvania Associators.

Following the fall of New York in the summer of 1776, Roberdeau and his Associators engaged the British in New Jersey. Said Roberdeau to his men in a speech made on August 19, 1776: "As it hath pleased Providence, for the exercise of our patience, and for the defense of that freedom which we inherit from the great Giver of all things, to call us from our families to the field; and as I have the honor of being your General officer, I trust you will take it well in me to endeavor to point out to you whatever appears necessary, either for your own particular good, or the more noble object — the good of all."

Roberdeau's ability to lead and motivate was widely evident. Unfortunately, he became ill and was evacuated to Lancaster, Pennsylvania to recover. Meanwhile, the Pennsylvania Associators disbanded following the Battles of Trenton and Princeton. The colony then formalized the Pennsylvania Militia in March 1777.

Recovered from his illness, Roberdeau was elected to the Continental Congress on February 5, 1777, serving for two years. During the winter of 1777/78, when General Washington was at Valley Forge, Roberdeau set up and commanded what became known as the Flying Camp, an attempt to rally and organize state militias to the cause. Ultimately, the Flying Camp concept gave way to a centralized Continental Army.

In November 1777, Roberdeau was among the Continental Congressman who adopted the Articles of Confederation. Sadly, wife Mary Roberdeau passed away this year.

In April 1778, Roberdeau decided to deal with the shortage of ammunition in the army and left Congress for several months on an expedition into western Pennsylvania at his own expense to discover and establish a lead mine in what is now Blair County. He also built a timber palisade fort to protect it that became known as Fort Roberdeau or "Lead Mine Fort."

Roberdeau married his second wife, Jane Milligan, on December 3, 1778, and the mine produced 1000 pounds of lead. The mine ran into

The grave of Daniel Roberdeau

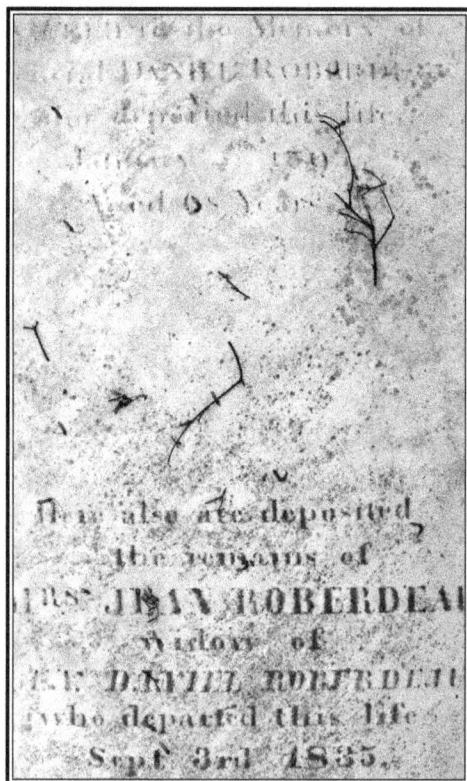

1780, when production halted, and the fort became a haven for local settlers.

Following the war, in 1783, Roberdeau traveled to England with his son, Isaac, to arrange his education. He then returned to Philadelphia in 1784, but did not stay long. Instead, he moved to Alexandria, Virginia, where he established a wharf and distillery.

As his health began to fail, Roberdeau moved to Winchester, Virginia, to be near his daughter. He died there on January 5, 1795. The *Aurora General Advertiser* of Philadelphia noted, "Died . . . in this town, on Monday last, after a lingering illness, which he bore with great Christian fortitude, and patient resignation to the Divine Will, General Daniel Roberdeau. He formerly resigned in Alexandria, and was a man universally esteemed, not only on account of the meritorious services [that] he rendered this country in a military capacity, but also for his strict integrity, piety, benevolence and philanthropy."

Roberdeau was buried in Mount Hebron Cemetery in Winchester.

Son Isaac Roberdeau was an Army officer and civil engineer who assisted Pierre L'Enfant with the plan for Washington, D.C.

Fort Roberdeau was reconstructed in the 1930s and remains a historic site near Altoona, Pennsylvania.

Charles Scott
(1739 – 1813)

Head of Intelligence

Buried at Frankfort Cemetery,
Frankfort, Kentucky.

———•—•———

Military • Political

Charles Scott was an early proponent of westward expansion and was best known as the fourth governor of Kentucky. Scott also served in the military for many years. He was a member of the ill-fated Braddock Expedition and then served in the American Revolution, ending the war as a major general. He was a trusted adviser to George Washington and handled his intelligence gathering. After the war, he accepted a grant of land in the west, settled there, and helped to quell the natives as a member of Anthony Wayne's Legion of the United States.

———•◦•———

Charles Scott was born in April 1739, in what was part of Goochland County, Virginia, now Powhatan County, to Samuel Scott, a farmer and member of the Virginia House of Burgesses, and his wife. Scott's mother likely died circa 1745, and her name is lost to history. Scott was the second of five children. He had an older brother, John, and younger siblings Edward, Joseph, and Martha. He did not receive much education.

Samuel Scott, a widower, died in 1755, leaving the five children as orphans. Charles apprenticed as a carpenter and was to be placed with a guardian by the court when, at 16, he enlisted in the Virginia Regiment. He was assigned to David Bell's company and rose to the rank of sergeant by the next year.

Charles Scott (1739 – 1813)

Charles Scott

During the Braddock Expedition and after, Scott served under George Washington, conducting scouting and escort missions. Scott was then part of the Forbes Expedition, after which Washington promoted him to ensign. Around 1759, Virginia's forces were switched to Colonel William Byrd. Scott was elevated to captain and led an expedition against the Cherokee. Before 1762, Scott left the military to return home.

Older brother John Scott died before 1762, making Charles the heir to his father's lands. Scott settled on his inherited farm and married Frances Sweeney of Cumberland County, Virginia, on February 25, 1762. Scott raised tobacco and milled flour with the help of his slaves. In 1766, he was named a captain in the local militia. He and Frances had eight or nine children over the years.

At the outset of the American Revolution, Scott was quick to serve, raising a company of volunteers in Cumberland County. The company was to aid Patrick Henry in a potential clash with Lord Dunmore in Williamsburg in May 1775, but Dunmore abandoned the city. Scott was made the temporary commander-in-chief of volunteers until he was elected a lieutenant colonel in William Woodford's regiment in August. His younger brother Joe served as a lieutenant in the same regiment. On December 9, 1775, this regiment helped win the Battle of Great Bridge, which stopped a British advance and led to the occupation of Norfolk. Lord Dunmore subsequently left Virginia.

In early 1776, the regiment was merged into the Continental Army, and Scott retained his rank. On August 12, 1776, the Continental Congress elevated Scott to colonel of the 5th Virginia Regiment under Adam Stephens, stationed at Hampton and Portsmouth, until Washington ordered them to New Jersey in the fall, where they participated in the successful Battle of Trenton on December 26. The following week, at the Battle of Assunpink Creek, the 5th Virginia slowed the advance of British and Hessian forces marching towards Trenton. A member of Scott's unit, Major George Johnston, later said Scott had "acquired immortal honor" for his performance.

While Washington camped at Morristown, New Jersey that winter, Scott was based at Chatham, from which he led raids on foraging parties. At the Battle of Drake's Farm on February 1, 1777, Scott defeated a superior force of British and Hessian mercenaries. On February 8, Scott's unit raided a force of over 2,000 soldiers at the Battle of Quibbletown, earning some note.

Scott was granted a furlough in the spring of 1777 and returned to his Virginia farm. While there, Congress promoted him to brigadier general. On May 10, 1777, Washington requested Scott's return to duty at Trenton. The following months were difficult for Washington and the Continental Army. At the Battle of Brandywine, Scott's 4th Virginia Brigade fought well against Cornwallis's advancing forces but had to retreat. British General Howe now advanced towards Philadelphia, stopping at Germantown. Scott urged an attack upon Germantown. Washington ultimately agreed, and the attack went forward on October 4, 1777. Scott's troops, however, were a non-factor. They became lost in smoke from muskets and a fire set by the British. Confused, the colonials retreated.

With Howe taking Philadelphia, Scott urged an attack on the capital but instead was ordered to engage in skirmishes near Whitemarsh. The army then settled in at Valley Forge for the winter. Scott stayed at Samuel Jones's farm and did not experience his men's difficulties in the camp. But he inspected the troops daily. Scott was again furloughed from March to May to return home to attend to his farm.

In June 1778, Washington ordered Scott to take 1500 troops and harass the British in New Jersey. He was joined by Marquis de Lafayette and 1000 more men. They expected to launch a major offensive the next day, but there was confusion under Major General Charles Lee's leadership, who oversaw the operation. After several days of delay, Lee finally launched the attack that became the Battle of Monmouth on June 28. However, the forces were not well-organized, and when an artillery unit was seen retreating, though they had only run out of ammunition, Scott ordered his men to retreat, and then other units followed. Lee aborted the offensive, greatly angering Washington, who arrived on the scene to stop the British advance. Lee was later court-martialed for his behavior and was suspended from command.

After Monmouth, the British retreated to New York City. Scott was made Washington's chief of intelligence and conducted scouting missions out of the base at White Plains, New York. There were no significant operations before Scott's furlough in November 1778.

The following spring, Scott was ordered to recruit volunteers. Washington's attention had turned south, and there was confusion about British intentions in Virginia. Scott was retained in Petersburg to defend Virginia should the British attack. By the spring of 1780, it was clear Charleston was the British target, and Scott was sent there just as Clinton laid siege to the city. Scott was captured when the city surrendered on May 12. He was then a prisoner. On January 30, 1781, citing poor health, Scott requested parole from General Cornwallis, who obliged his request. Scott was out of action until he was exchanged for Lord Rawdon in July 1782, missing the Battle of Yorktown.

Washington next sent Scott to assist Peter Muhlenberg in recruiting troops in Virginia. He was then told to report to General Nathanael Greene, but Greene wrote he did not have a position for him and urged him to stay with Muhlenberg. The peace treaty ending the war was signed in March 1783. Scott was brevetted to major general on September 30,

1783, just before leaving the army. He then became a founding member of the Society of the Cincinnati.

Scott, like many soldiers, was granted land in the west by the Virginia legislature. Scott was given over 20,000 acres in Fayette and Bourbon counties. He spent the next two years preparing to settle along the Kentucky River in what would later become the state of Kentucky. In 1787, Scott moved his family to their new plantation near Versailles. He constructed a two-story log cabin and stockade and prepared to raise tobacco. That June, within weeks of moving, Shawnee warriors killed and scalped his son, Samuel, while crossing the Ohio River in a canoe. He watched helplessly from the riverbank. According to later biographers, this was the incentive for Scott's harsh treatment of the natives after that. Scott focused on building his plantation and served one term in the Virginia House of Burgesses.

In 1790, during the early days of the Washington administration, tensions increased with the natives in the Northwest Territory. Scott raised volunteers in Fayette and Bourbon counties to assist Josiah Harmar in a raid against the Western Confederacy. This expedition fought some skirmishes but accomplished little. In June, Harmar and Arthur St. Clair were ordered to lead another expedition against the Indians. Scott did not participate due to his service in the Virginia General Assembly. The expedition failed, and there was great distrust of Harmar among the Kentuckians.

On December 30, 1790, concerned about the failed expeditions, Washington urged Virginia's Governor Randolph to appoint Scott the general overseeing the Kentucky district. The next month, Scott was included in the Kentucky Board of War, which also comprised Senator John Brown, Isaac Shelby, Harry Innes, and Benjamin Logan. They urged a campaign against the Indians along the Ohio River. Washington agreed but selected Arthur St. Clair to lead, much to the disappointment of the Kentuckians. Scott was asked to lead 1000 men under St. Clair, about one-third of the force. Before launching the primary attack, Scott was ordered to take his men and distract the Indians while the main force gathered. He did so, capturing or killing nearly 100 Indians while only losing two men, who drowned in a river crossing. Scott's unit was then discharged.

Encouraged by Scott's prior success in the Wabash region, St. Clair encouraged the Board of War to mount another expedition on June 24, 1791. This time, Scott designated others to mount the raids, which were successful, taking a heavy toll on the Indians. The Weas and Kickapoos later signed a peace treaty in 1792 and moved further west.

St. Clair intended to mount a large initiative despite the Kentuckians' reluctance, many of whom were resisting service. Scott set about recruiting men for St. Clair. Colonel William Oldham was the highest-ranking of the Kentuckians. St. Clair's party headed out on October 1. On November 3, after setting camp, they were attacked before dawn by Indians. Of St. Clair's 1400 men, 600 were killed and 300 captured. St. Clair retreated and was joined by Scott and 200 volunteers. However, Scott's men did not have to fight as the Indians did not attack again. The natives' success further emboldened other tribes in the region.

President Washington now called for creating a 5000-man Legion of the United States to fight the Indians in the Northwest Territory. He considered assigning his friend Scott to lead the legion but decided against it because of Scott's penchant for alcohol. Instead, Washington appointed Anthony Wayne. On June 1, 1792, Kentucky became a state. Three days later, Scott and Benjamin Logan were appointed Major Generals of the state militia. Scott was given responsibility for territory north of the Kentucky River. During this time, there was discussion of Scott running for Congress, but he served only as a presidential elector in 1793.

Wayne arrived in mid-1793 with only 3000 of the 5000 men he intended. Scott's force was merged into the federal army, and Scott was commissioned an officer. However, the rest of the year, there was no significant action, and the men went home for the winter. The following spring, Wayne built Fort Recovery in Kentucky on the site of St. Clair's defeat. This helped raise the Kentuckians' confidence in their federal commander, especially when Wayne had 600 skulls the Indians had dug up reburied.

In June 1794, Wayne built Fort Defiance on an abandoned Indian town. Scott had a role in naming it, saying, "I defy the English, Indians, and all the devils in hell to take it." Wayne then marched to Fort Miami, where he expected to fight the Indians and British. On August 20,

Wayne's forces engaged with the Indians at the Battle of Fallen Timbers. The Indians were routed, and the British refused to open their fort to the natives. The campaign ended two months later, in October. The House of Representatives, while commending Wayne on December 4, 1794, thanked Scott for his service. The Treaty of Greenville ended the war in 1795.

For the rest of the 1790s, Scott served as the major general of the 2nd division of state militia. He was highly regarded as a military hero in Kentucky. His daughter Martha married future US Senator George M. Bibb in 1799. In 1800 and 1804, he again functioned as a presidential elector, voting for Democratic-Republicans. Scott's wife, Martha, died on October 6, 1804, after which he sold his farm and moved in with his daughter and son in law in Lexington.

In 1807, as tensions mounted with Great Britain following the Chesapeake-Leopard Affair, Scott suggested to Governor Christopher Greenup that he should raise a mounted militia unit. The governor agreed, but Scott remarried on July 25, 1807, Judith Cary (Bell) Gist and did not assemble the unit. Gist was the widow of an old friend from the Revolution, Colonel Nathaniel Gist. Scott and his new wife settled at Canewood, the Gist family plantation.

On February 11, 1808, Scott announced his candidacy for the governorship of Kentucky. His stepson-in-law, Jess Bledsoe, a law professor at Transylvania University, managed the campaign. As the most senior Revolutionary War officer in the state, Scott controlled the veterans' lobby, boosting his candidacy. He won the campaign by a nearly two-to-one margin over his two opponents.

Upon taking the governorship, Scott appointed Bledsoe his Secretary of State. It was Bledsoe who delivered Scott's address to the legislature on December 13, 1808. Later that winter, Scott slipped on the icy steps of the governor's mansion and was permanently injured, requiring crutches for the rest of his life. This made him more dependent on his Secretary of State, who performed many of his official functions.

Rumors of alcoholism followed Scott during his term as governor. He was known to drink heavily and use profanity profusely. On one occasion, while providing feedback on a speech written by Bledsoe, Scott remarked, "Well, Mr. Bledsoe, I know you think you are a damned sight smarter than I am, and so you are in many respects; but this message as it is now, won't do at all; I'll be damned if it will." After Bledsoe asked what was wrong with the speech, Scott replied, "Why, damn it to hell, why don't you put a good solemn prayer at the end of it, and talk about Providence, and the protection of Heaven, and all that?"

As war with Britain again loomed, Scott was a staunch supporter. He backed William Henry Harrison's recruitment of Kentuckians who ultimately fought at the Battle of Tippecanoe. Scott used the newspapers to call for volunteers to fight the British. On August 14, 1812, Scott greeted two regiments at the governor's mansion. As he hobbled among the soldiers with his crutch, he hammered it against the steps and said, "If it hadn't been for you (the crutch), I could have gone with the boys myself." On his last day in office, August 25, Scott made Harrison major general over the Kentucky militia, even though Harrison was not a

The weathered stone of Charles Scott.

resident. While unconstitutional, it was a popular move. President James Madison soon made Harrison the supreme commander of the Army of the Northwest.

His term over, Scott retired to Canewood with his wife. By mid-1813, Scott's health began to fail. He died on October 22, 1813 and was initially buried at Canewood. His remains were reinterred at Frankfort Cemetery in 1854. During the ceremony in 1854, a speaker described Scott as "a man of strong natural powers, faithful and constant in his friendships and implacable in his enmities. Somewhat illiterate, he was unpolished in manners and very eccentric."

Scott counties in Kentucky and Indiana are named after Charles Scott. Scottsville, Kentucky, and Scottsville, Virginia, are also named in his honor.

George Wythe
(1726 – 1806)

The Law Professor

Buried at St. John's Episcopal Churchyard,
Richmond, Virginia.

———•◦•———

Declaration of Independence

George Wythe was at one time the most respected and revered man in Virginia if not in the whole United States. He was America's first law professor and a close friend and mentor of Thomas Jefferson, James Monroe, John Marshall, and Henry Clay. He was a signer of the Declaration of Independence and a delegate to the 1787 Philadelphia Convention. He left the convention before the signing of the U.S. Constitution to tend to his dying wife. He played an important role at the Virginia Ratifying Convention and over the years grew to hate slavery and freed his slaves. He was murdered by his great-nephew George Sweeney in 1806 although Sweeney was found "not guilty" when tried.

———➤•◦•◄———

It all began in 1726 when George Wythe was born in what is now Hampton, Virginia. His father died when he was three. His mother Margaret Walker Wythe instilled in him a love of learning and home-schooled him until he was sixteen. At that age, he began to study law in the office of his uncle Stephen Dewey. George was admitted to the bar in 1746 the same year his mother died. Early in 1748, he married Ann Lewis, who died eight months later. The bereaved widower settled in Williamsburg to teach and practice law.

Etching of George Wythe by an unknown artist.

Wythe got his first taste of public service in 1748 when he was appointed a clerk for two important committees of the House of Burgess. In 1750 he was elected a Williamsburg alderman and in 1754 elected to the House of Burgess.

Shortly after in 1755, he married Elizabeth Taliaferro. Her father Richard built them a house in Williamsburg which is still called the George Wythe House and is open to the public.

In 1762 a college professor friend William Small introduced Wythe to Thomas Jefferson and suggested Wythe supervise Jefferson's legal training. He agreed and a lifelong friendship ensued. Wythe continued his thriving legal practice with Jefferson's assistance and in 1767, Wythe introduced Jefferson to the bar of the General Court, and he himself was appointed as clerk to the House of Burgess.

In 1764, Wythe wrote the original Virginia protest against the Stamp Act. It was so fiery that it had to be rewritten in a softer tone to gain approval. It didn't hurt his popularity however as he was elected Mayor of Williamsburg in 1768.

On May 10, 1775, the Second Continental Congress convened in Philadelphia. Wythe was elected as a delegate to replace George Washington, who took command of the continental army. He was very active at the Congress and voted for the Declaration of Independence. The historic document was not ready for signing until August 2 and by that time Wythe had returned to Williamsburg, thus he and other absent delegates signed later. He signed the document in September. His signature appears first among the Virginia signatures. He was so highly respected by his fellow Virginians that the other delegates left a space so that his signature would be first. The signers' names were not made public until the following January, for all knew the Declaration was an act of treason, punishable by death.

Wythe taught for over twenty years at the College of William and Mary. In 1779, Wythe was appointed to the nation's first law professorship, established at the college by his former student Thomas Jefferson.

In 1787 Wythe became one of Virginia's delegates to the Constitutional Convention. He, Alexander Hamilton, and Charles Pinckney served on the committee which established the Convention's rules and procedures. He left the Convention early before the signing took place to tend to his dying wife Elizabeth. She died later that year.

The following year, he was one of the Federalist leaders at the Virginia Ratifying Convention. There he presided over the Committee of the Whole and offered the resolution for ratification. He helped to sway the delegates to support the new constitution and Virginia narrowly became the tenth state to ratify it.

Over the years Wythe had grown to hate slavery, and after his second wife Elizabeth died, he began to free his slaves. He lived with two of his former slaves: a housekeeper Lydia Broadnax, and a young man named Michael Brown. Wythe was so fond of Michael that he named him to inherit a part of his estate. Also living with him was his great-nephew, George Wythe Sweeney. Sweeney, who was in line to inherit most of the estate was a ne'er-do-well who ran up huge gambling debts and had forged his uncle's name on checks and stolen from him to cover his debts. Hoping to avoid detection and inherit the entire estate, he resorted to murder. He poisoned coffee, most probably with arsenic, that George Wythe, Michael Brown, and Lydia Broadnax drank. George and Michael both died from the poison but Lydia survived. Sweeney was indicted for murder. There was plenty of evidence against Sweeney, but by Virginia law, blacks could not testify against whites in court, so Lydia was not heard, and Sweeney was found "not guilty" of murder. Wythe died a slow and painful death on June 8, 1806.

Wythe's funeral was the largest in state history until that time. Richmond businesses closed for the day, and thousands lined the funeral route. The service was conducted at the state capitol. He was buried at St. John's Episcopal Churchyard in Richmond, the church in which Patrick Henry made his famous "give me liberty or give me death" speech.

In his will, Wythe left his large book collection to Thomas Jefferson which he later sold to create the Library of Congress. There is a Wythe Avenue in Richmond and the law school at the College of William and Mary is named the Marshall-Wythe School of Law. His home in Williamsburg, as previously mentioned, operates as a museum.

Grave of George Wythe in Saint Johns Episcopal
Churchyard in Richmond, Virginia
(photo by Lawrence Knorr).

Sources

Books, Magazines, Journals, Files:

Alexander, Edward P. *Revolutionary Conservative: James Duane of New York*. New York: Ams Press, 1978.

Anthony, Katharine Susan. *First Lady of the Revolution; The Life of Mercy Otis Warren*. Port Washington, N.Y.: Kennikat Press, 1972.

Appleby, Joyce. *Inheriting the Revolution: The First Generation of Americans*. Cambridge, Massachusetts: Harvard University Press, 2000.

Atkinson, Rick. *The British Are Coming: The War for America, Lexington to Princeton, 1775–1777*. New York: Henry Holt & Co. 2019.

Bordewich, Fergus M. *The First Congress: How James Madison, George Washington, and a Group of Extraordinary Men Invented the Government*. New York: Simon and Schuster Paperbacks, 2016.

Boudreau, George W. *Independence: A Guide to Historic Philadelphia*. Yardley, Pennsylvania: Westholme Publishing, LLC. 2012.

Bowen, Catherine Drinker. *Miracle at Philadelphia: The Story of the Constitutional Convention May to September 1787*. Boston, Massachusetts: Little, Brown & Company, 1966.

Breen, T.H, *George Washington's Journey: The President Forges a New Nation*. New York: Simon & Schuster. 2016.

Brookhiser, Richard. *Gentleman Revolutionary: Gouverneur Morris The Rake Who Wrote the Constitution*. New York: Free Press, 2003.

———. *John Marshall: The Man Who Made the Supreme Court*. New York: Basic Books. 2018.

Brush, Edward Hale. *Rufus King and His Times*. New York: N.L. Brown, 1926.

Chadwick, Bruce. I Am Murdered: *George Wythe, Thomas Jefferson, and the Killing That Shocked a New Nation*. Hoboken, New Jersey: John Wiley & Sons, 2009.

Chambers, II, John Whiteclay. *The Oxford Companion to American Military History*. Oxford: Oxford University Press, 1999.

Commager, Henry Steele & Richard B. Morris. *The Spirit of 'Seventy-Six: The Story of the American Revolution as Told by Participants*. New York: Harper & Rowe, 1967.

Cole, Ryan. *Light-Horse Harry Lee: The Rise and Fall of a Revolutionary Hero*. Washington, D.C.: Regnery History. 2019.

Conlin, Joseph R. *The Morrow Book of Quotations in American History*. New York: William Morrow and Company, Inc., 1984.

Daniels, Jonathan. *Ordeal of Ambition*. Garden City, New York: Doubleday & Company, Inc., 1970.

Dann, John C. *The Revolution Remembered: Eyewitness Accounts of the War for Independence*. Chicago: University of Chicago Press, 1980.

DeRose, Chris. *Founding Rivals: Madison vs. Monroe: The Bill of Rights and the Election that Saved a Nation.* New York: MJF Books, 2011.

Drury, Bob & Tom Clavin. *Valley Forge.* New York: Simon & Schuster. 2018.

Ellis, Joseph J. *Revolutionary Summer: The Birth of American Independence.* New York: Alfred A. Knopf, 2013.

———. *The Quartet: Orchestrating the Second American Revolution, 1783–1789.* New York: Alfred A. Knopf, 2015.

———. *His Excellency: George Washington.* New York: Alfred A. Knopf, 2004.

Flexner, James Thomas. *George Washington in the American Revolution, 1775–1783.* Boston: Little, Brown & Company, 1967.

Flower, Lenore Embick. "Visit of President George Washington to Carlisle, 1794." Carlisle, Pennsylvania: The Hamilton Library and Cumberland County Historical Society, 1932.

Gerlach, Don R. *Proud Patriot: Philip Schuyler and the War of Independence, 1775–1783.* Syracuse, N.Y.: Syracuse University Press, 1987.

Goodrich, Charles A. *Lives of the Signers of the Declaration of Independence.* Charlotteville, N.Y.: SamHar Press, 1976.

Griffith, IV, William R. *The Battle of Lake George: England's First Triumph in the French and Indian War.* Charleston, South Carolina: The History Press, 2016.

Grossman, Mark. *Encyclopedia of the Continental Congress.* Armenia, New York: Grey House Publishing, 2015.

Hamilton, Edward P. *Fort Ticonderoga: Key to a Continent.* Boston: Little, Brown & Company, 1964.

Isenberg, Nancy. *Fallen Founder: The Life of Aaron Burr.* New York: Penguin Group, 2007.

Kennedy, Roger G. *Burr, Hamilton, and Jefferson: A Study in Character.* New York: Oxford University Press, 1999.

Kiernan, Denise & Joseph D'Agnese. *Signing Their Lives Away: The Fame and Misfortune of the Men Who Signed the Declaration of Independence.* Philadelphia: Quirk Books, 2008.

———. *Signing Their Rights Away: The Fame and Misfortune of the Men Who Signed the United States Constitution.* Philadelphia: Quirk Books, 2011.

Klarman, Michael J. *The Framers' Coup: The Making of the United States Constitution.* New York: Oxford University Press, 2016.

Langguth, A. J. *Patriots.* New York: Simon and Schuster, 1988.

Larson, Edward J. *A Magnificent Catastrophe.* New York: Free Press, 2007.

Lee, Mike. Written *Out of History: The Forgotten Founders Who Fought Big Government.* New York: Penguin Books, 2017.

Lewis, James E., Jr., *The Burr Conspiracy: Uncovering the Story of an Early American Crisis,* Princeton: Princeton University Press, 2017.

Lockridge, Ross Franklin. *The Harrisons.* 1941.

Lomask, Milton. *Aaron Burr: The Years from Princeton to Vice President, 1756–1805.* New York: Farrar Straus Giroux, 1979.

Lossing, Benson J. *Pictorial Field Book of the Revolution.* New York: Harper Brothers. 1851.

SOURCES

Maier, Pauline. *American Scripture: Making the Declaration of Independence.* New York: Alfred A. Knopf, Inc., 1997.

McCullough, David. *John Adams.* New York: Simon & Schuster, 2002.

Meltzer, Brad & Josh Mensch. *The First Conspiracy: The Secret Plot to Kill George Washington.* New York: Flat Iron Books. 2018.

Middlekauff, Robert. *The Glorious Cause: The American Revolution, 1763–1789.* Oxford: Oxford University Press, 2005.

Miller, Jr., Arthur P. & Marjorie L. Miller. *Pennsylvania Battlefields and Military Landmarks.* Mechanicsburg, Pennsylvania: Stackpole Books, 2000.

Millett, Allan R. & Peter Maslowski. *For the Common Defense: A Military History of the United States of America.* New York: The Free Press, 1984.

Moore, Charles. *The Family Life of George Washington.* New York: Houghton Mifflin, 1926.

Nagel, Paul C. *The Lees of Virginia: Seven Generations of an American Family.* Oxford: Oxford University Press, 1990.

O'Connell, Robert L. *Revolutionary: George Washington at War.* New York: Random House. 2019.

Racove, Jack N. *Revolutionaries: A New History of the Invention of America.* New York: Houghton Mifflin Harcourt, 2011.

Raphael, Ray. Founding Myths: *Stories That Hide Our Patriotic Past.* New York: MJF Books, 2004.

Rossiter, Clinton. *1787 The Grand Convention.* New York: The Macmillan Company, 1966.

Seymour, Joseph. *The Pennsylvania Associators, 1747–1777.* Yardley, Pennsylvania: Westholme Publishing, LLC. 2012.

Schweikart, Larry & Michael Allen. *A Patriot's History of the United States from Columbus's Great Discovery to the War on Terror.* New York: Penguin, 2004.

Sharp, Arthur G. *Not Your Father's Founders.* Avon, Massachusetts: Adams Media, 2012.

Stahr, Walter. *John Jay: Founding Father.* New York: Diversion Books, 2017.

Taafee, Stephen R. *The Philadelphia Campaign, 1777–1778.* Lawrence, Kansas: University of Kansas Press, 2003.

Tinkcom, Harry Marlin, *The Republicans and the Federalists in Pennsylvania, 1790–1801.* Harrisburg, Pennsylvania: Pennsylvania Historical and Museum Commission. 1950.

Ward, Matthew C. *Breaking the Backcountry: The Seven Years' War in Virginia and Pennsylvania, 1754–1765.* Pittsburgh, Pennsylvania: University of Pittsburgh Press, 2003.

Weisberger, Bernard A. *America Afire: Jefferson, Adams, and the Revolutionary Election of 1800.* New York: HarperCollins, 2000.

Wood, Gordon S. *The Radicalism of the American Revolution.* New York: Vintage Books, 1993.

———. *Empire of Liberty: A History of the Early Republic, 1789–1815.* New York: Penguin Books, 2004.

———. *Revolutionary Characters: What Made the Founders Different.* New York: Penguin Books, 2006.

————. *The Americanization of Benjamin Franklin*. Oxford: Oxford University Press, 2009.

Wright, Benjamin F. *The Federalist: The Famous Papers on the Principles of American Government: Alexander Hamilton, James Madison, John Jay*. New York: Metro Books, 2002.

Zobel, Hiller B. *The Boston Massacre*. New York: W. W. Norton & Company, 1970.

Video Resources:

Guelzo, Allen C. The Great Courses: *America's Founding Fathers* (Course N. 8525). Chantilly, Virginia: The Teaching Company, 2017.

Online Resources:

Archives.gov – for information on the Constitutional Convention.

CauseofLiberty.blogspot.com – for information on Daniel Carroll.

ColonialHall.com – for information about the signers of the Declaration of Independence.

DSDI1776.com – for information on many Founders.

FamousAmericans.net – for information on many Founders.

FindaGrave.com – for burial information, vital statistics and obituaries.

FirstLadies.org – for information on Abigail Adams.

Newspapers.com – Hundreds of newspaper articles were accessed—too numerous to mention here.

NPS.gov – for information on various park sites.

TeachingAmericanHistory.com – for information on Charles Pinckney and George Wythe.

TheHistoryJunkie.com – for information on multiple Founders.

USHistory.org – for information on multiple Founders.

Wikipedia.com – for general historical information.

Index

INDEX

VIRGINIA PATRIOTS

INDEX

INDEX

INDEX

www.ingramcontent.com/pod-product-compliance
Lightning Source LLC
Chambersburg PA
CBHW021225090426
42740CB00006B/389